Why
I DON'T TAKE
Milk
IN MY
Tea

*How I remember my young life and
the people who shared my world*

JENNIFER ROWE

BALBOA.PRESS

A DIVISION OF HAY HOUSE

Balboa Press books may be ordered through booksellers or by contacting:

Balboa Press
A Division of Hay House
1663 Liberty Drive
Bloomington, IN 47403
www.balboapress.com.au
AU TFN: 1 800 844 925 (Toll Free inside Australia)
AU Local: 0283 107 086 (+61 2 8310 7086 from outside Australia)

Print information available on the last page.

ISBN: 978-1-5043-2189-1 (sc)
ISBN: 978-1-5043-2190-7 (e)

Balboa Press rev. date: 07/21/2020

Stories of my young life growing up in Fleetwood, a small fishing town. With a splash of family history and some ancestors to sweeten the brew

Jennifer Rowe

"I want my children and grandchildren to remember me warts and all, but most of all for the love I have for them, my family, my world."

Author Jennifer Rowe

CONTENTS

PART TWO

Stories of my ancestors and their link to Fleetwood

PREFACE

"Telling our personal story constitutes an act of consciousness that defines the ethical lining of a person's constitution. Recounting personal stories promotes personal growth, spurs the performance of selfless deeds, and in doing so enhances the ability of the equitable eye of humanity to scroll rearward and forward. Every person must become familiar with our communal history of struggle, loss, redemption, and meaningfully contemplate the meaning behind our personal existence in order to draft a proper and prosperous future for succeeding generations. Accordingly, every person is responsible for sharing their story using the language of thought that best expresses their sanguine reminiscences. Without a record of pastimes, we will never know what we were, what we now are, or what we might become by steadfastly and honourably struggling with mortal chores"

Kilroy J. Oldster, Dead Toad Scrolls

I WANTED TO WRITE THIS book for my family, to share with them the life I lived before they entered into it, and commit to memory their early years. It is important to me they have knowledge and understanding of a life they had no part of, but of one in which I emerged loved and happy. My interest in genealogy inspired me to write my story, it made me aware of how little I knew about the family who surrounded my upbringing, and the family that had lived a few hundred years before me. Their stories made visible people who had faced heartbreak, who had worked hard, and above all had survived the adversity in their lives. As I started to unravel their lives, I realized that some of their stories mirrored my own life in many ways, especially those pertaining to the sea, so I have included some of their stories as a record for my family, who I am sure will be amazed at the similarities, of our situations.

The book is about my memories growing up in the seaside town of Fleetwood in Lancashire which was once a thriving fishing port. I was born in 1948 and those times were very different from today, just as times were different for my ancestor's. The best part about writing this book was having to recall as much as I could about my life, which stirred up memories I had long forgotten, or had been skewed to make them more palatable. It has also been an emotional journey, as many memories remain raw to me, but I have faced them with honesty and criticism with that familiar "I wish I had done things differently" feeling in the background.

We left Fleetwood in 1969 emigrating to New Zealand and a new life, and this is when a new beginning for our own children started. I can't pretend it was easy to bring up children in a foreign country with no family around us, but I know they would not think their lives lacking because of this fact. We had to "stick together" as a family leading to a closeness I still cherish. We were lucky to have been able to travel back to England on a few occasions which enabled our children to be part of their Fleetwood family's lives, even for a short period of time. I am grateful to my sisters Janet and Margaret who never forgot my children, and have kept them part of their distanced lives for many years. To this day their love for my children and grandchildren never wavers, and they are still a big part of our lives.

I dedicate this book to my Mum and Dad's memory, taken far too young from my life, but who left me with a legacy of love and courage that underpins the life I lead now. I feel sad they were not able to have many years together, to see their family grow up, and to have the love of grandchildren as I do. I am however grateful in my lifetime to have shared over fifty-five years with the love of my life, and bared witness to those events my Mum and Dad never had a chance to experience. Thanks Dave, for being patient and understanding of my time whilst writing this story, also for the many cups of tea and for listening to parts of the text over and over, but that's what you have done so well over the years.

INTRODUCTION

I STARTED THIS BOOK WHEN I was sixty-three years old and I am now seventy-two and beginning to think I may not get it finished before old age takes its toll on arthritic fingers and a memory which already shows signs of forgetfulness. I will not be deterred though; I am a tough cookie and a finisher so there are at least two attributes I can call on to help me with this task. I call it a task but really it is a passion, it has helped me to connect to my childhood, my dearly loved Mum and Dad, and the happy days with my brothers and sisters. I'm not really sure why I started to think about my past having never been slightly interested in it before, but when I started to do genealogy I began to think about my own life as a youngster. At this point it was blatantly obvious that I really knew very little about my family, let alone my ancestors. Perhaps my age has something to do with it, I don't know, but I do wish I had thought about my family and ancestors thirty years ago when there were people alive to answer the many questions I had, but then thirty years ago I wasn't interested and wouldn't have known what to ask anyway. Maybe I have been guided to embark on this voyage of discovery, maybe my curiosity has just got the better of me, who knows, but whatever the reason, I now have the confidence and interest to begin my journey. In the beginning I really wanted to document the life of my ancestors' not so much about my life, but as I started to write it became clear that my ancestors' and I are intertwined, having passed on DNA from generation to generation just as my own DNA is on its journey through my own family. It is the lives they lived before me that has shaped my early beginnings, so it was inevitable and obvious that the key part of this book should be about my life. So, I started with very little knowledge about those family members who influenced me in some way, but each tiny fragment of information has guided me to research further. It was almost as if I was being driven to find out more and more, as if my ancestors were saying yes keep searching, you are on the right path.

When I started my book, I was blessed with two elderly aunts who tried to answer my many questions, they had to think back many years to unlock their pasts which left us to laugh a little and to cry a lot. Aunty Myra was my mother's youngest sister and she tried hard to help me sort out the little-known facts about the maternal side of my family but I have a feeling like me, she never asked many questions either. I don't know where my Mum and Dad met or details such as how long they had known each other or if it was love at first sight. I also knew nothing about my grandparents only my Mums mother, Nan, who played such a big part in our lives. Aunty Beat was my Dad's sister, fortunately she was able to give me snippets of information about my Dad's side of the family which helped me to untangle some amazing facts about the paternal side of my family, giving me a little insight into their lives. I watched both my aunties trying hard to remember dates, places, and people, and their recollections are the precursor to begin my story, how grateful I am to them both for their influence. Sadly, they have both now passed away, so I am here today with no older members of the family left to answer my many questions. It is a task that sometimes feels overwhelming, as I embark on a journey of discovery and candour, with memories that are both sad and happy, but nevertheless are mine to share and keep forever.

As I have said before I never asked any questions about our family, but I am not on my own in this regard as many of my family and friends say the same thing. I can however make some educated assumptions about our family and their existence on this earth, and have tried to see through their eyes the social and economic times they lived in, and the circumstances which would have impacted on their lives. My journey has also taken me back to my beloved Fleetwood, the town where I was born and brought up, where my early years evoke such happy memories. I left Fleetwood with no regrets when I was twenty-one and have now nearly fifty years later reconnected to a history that I wish I hadn't abandoned for all those years. There is something about Fleetwood that makes it so special and I think it is the people who were born and bred there, who understand the ethos of the town. These people have experienced the town's dramatic change from a thriving fishing port to one of unemployment with all it entails. They can also remember the kindness of neighbours, the busy port and the many shops that supplied all our needs. It was a town that understood the loneliness experienced when your men were out at sea, it was a town that mourned with you when those men didn't return. It was a town that did its best. With this understanding there comes a loyalty between the *born and breds* who will always have Fleetwood in their hearts and fiercely protect its heritage.

I do take comfort in the fact that I have managed to document many facts about our ancestors for my Fleetwood extended family to hopefully enjoy and appreciate. The end chapter is a must read for anyone starting to pursue their family history. I have written stories about my ancestors and they are a good example of what you can achieve once you start your research. Remember I didn't know anything at all about the family and I started with only Mum and Dad's wedding certificate and my grandfathers birth certificate. For those that don't want to research just read their stories anyway. They are sad and give you an idea of what it was like to live in times which seemed harsh for many. These discoveries have given me a connection to my ancestors whose feet have walked the pavements I have walked, played in the places I have played, and who have faced the same adversities my family faced, so maybe now I can be forgiven for this abandonment. Fleetwood is my town and I will always want it to be remembered as such, even though my own family live on the other side of the world. Some of my memories are very short, so there may be only one sentence, some of my memories are painful which I will share, but many of my childhood memories are happy and remind me of what a loved family we were. I can now appreciate how hard it was for my Mum and Dad to provide for six children, what a grand job they did with so little money. How did my Mum survive after being made a widow at thirty-five with six children to feed and clothe, how did she pick up her life again? How did I fall in love when I was fifteen, marry at sixteen and have a child when I had just turned seventeen? What made us emigrate to New Zealand, where did we live, how did we manage on our own? There are many questions to ask and answer, and my family may even know the answers to these questions as I have talked about my past often, but hopefully they will now be on record.

The past has shaped my life in times of happiness and sadness but that is life, that is how we learn, you just have to get on with it like so many who came before us had to. It does encourage a determination to do better though, not necessarily better than our parents, but to give us the right tools and strength to succeed in whichever path we wish to walk down. It encourages us to respect and care for each other, it gives us understanding of each other and it gives us our future. Although this is my story it is really the family story and even though my memories are at risk of slipping away as only night into day can, I have done the legwork, I have left a record of my life, a rich life that hopefully will be passed from generation to generation. I have only documented my life up to the time of our emigration to New Zealand and those early years following this so my children can connect with the memories of their childhood, after all this book is really for them.

CHAPTER ONE

The Beginning

"The beginning is the most important part of the work"
Plato, The Republic

MY NAME IS JENNIFER MARY Rowe nee Gorst and I was born on the 13 January, 1948 at 84 Warren Street, Fleetwood, Lancashire. I was the second child of Jim and Kathleen, and my eldest sister, Janet, was born on the 5th May, 1946. I don't know anything about my arrival, but I do know it would have been a cold winter day. Apparently, it was very windy and raining heavily. I would have been born either in our front room, known as the parlour in those days, or in Mum's bedroom. I think it would have been the parlour because a fire would have been burning and it would have been easier for the family to look after Mum, as in those days you stayed in bed for ten to fourteen days after having a baby. Nearly every house had a parlour which was always kept tidy and used for special occasions. If anyone came to visit who was worthy, they would be taken into the parlour. I'm not sure what the definition of worthy was in those days, but it certainly wasn't your run-of-the-mill relatives or friends. I have no idea how much I weighed or at what time I was born or if my Mum had any problems giving birth to me, and it would have been interesting to know. I also wonder how they felt about having another daughter, "were they thrilled, or disappointed?" I could ask so many questions now, but regrettably, there is no one to answer them anymore. I know sadly these and many more details have gone, buried in the graves of all my relatives who were part of my life.

I believe Sister Cross delivered me, not that I have proof of this but because she was the midwife in our area at that time. She must have been kept busy delivering babies at home, and in an age of no real contraception, there would have been many. It must also have been very scary to deliver babies at home, and when I look at my ancestors' lives there were many babies in our family that had died at birth. The practice of home deliveries went on for many years though, probably into the mid 1960s. I can remember my Mum helping the midwife when any of her neighbours went into labour, and she could always be relied on. It was quite acceptable for neighbours to help out, even if it was only to be on hand in case there were any complications and help had to be summoned. They didn't have a mobile phone, and most homes were without a telephone. In our neighbourhood, the phone box was five minutes away - and that was if you were running.

I think Dad may have been home for my birth. I know for sure he wouldn't have been present, because in those days' husbands were not allowed, and in all honesty, they probably didn't want to be. I have established through Dad's logbook that he was sailing in the trawler *Sethon* at that time and he signed off the trawler on the day I was born. Although I don't know the time I was born or any other details, it is comforting to think my Dad saw me on the first day of my life. Being the second child of six children, I can vaguely remember my brothers and sisters being born, as we were always sent to one of our aunties to be looked after when Mum went into labour. This was a real treat for us, as they were kind and looked after us well. I do remember the midwife bringing a box to our home a few weeks before the baby was due, and in the early days I use to think it was the baby being delivered to us. The box fascinated me, but it was kept secreted away under the bed and was not to be touched. When the baby was born the box would disappear like magic a few days later, as it was no longer needed. No one told me what was in the box; it was never explained to me, but that was usual for those times- if you were told no then it was a no and not for discussion. "A very different viewpoint from today," I hear you say. Nowadays people would think it unfair and not right that my question wasn't answered, but really it did me no harm, and I grew up okay and normal. I now know the box was a delivery box which would have held everything for the birth and early care of a newborn, such as sterile gloves, gauze pads, drop cloths, and waterproof covers for the bed, but definitely no baby. How could I think there was a baby in the box? But then, how could I believe that Father Christmas delivered toys to all the children in the world and worked throughout the night to get them delivered in time for Christmas morning? Such is the magic of childhood.

Warren Street had three bedrooms and no bathroom. The toilet was at the bottom of the yard and it had a wooden seat. On the wall there was a hook holding squares of newspaper which were used to wipe our bottoms on. Those families that had more money used a toilet paper called Izal, a little bit gentler but really, not that much better. We all slept in the front bedroom of the house in two large double beds with an eiderdown on each. In the middle of winter, when the ice was on the inside of the window, we had to use our coats as blankets to keep warm. I can't really remember having nice sheets and pillowcases, but I guess that wasn't important to us in those days. The floor was wooden with a rug which had been made by Nan; it was quite colourful, and I think it was made out of rags. There was also a huge double wardrobe in the room, but no dressing table. We had the basics and we knew nothing else. We never had any comparisons to make us discontented, so we were quite happy. My most special memory of that bedroom was this: on one Christmas Eve, we had been in bed for some time, trying hard to get to sleep so the morning would come quicker. Mum came into the room and told us to quickly get out of bed so we could see Father Christmas travelling on his sleigh. We all fell out of bed, rushed to the window, and huddled together to watch his sleigh flying through the dark sky. There was a lot of pushing and shoving of each other whilst trying to get the best view we could. We peered into the night sky with anticipation, scanning the stars which had lit up the sky, our excited breaths fogging the glass, which Mum had to keep on wiping. We saw a red-light flashing, which we all thought was Rudolf's nose, and we were thrilled as we watched his sleigh fly over us. If we had any doubts about Father Christmas, they vanished that night, and it was a long time before we realized Father Christmas's sleigh was an aeroplane. Mum was lucky to have spotted the plane that night, as it was unusual in those early days to see many aeroplanes in the sky, and she was so clever to make that moment a memory which has lasted throughout the decades.

We didn't have a bathroom, so we all had to have a "strip" wash in the kitchen every night and a bath once a week. The tin bath would be put in front of the fire and filled with hot water from the kettle, which as you can imagine was a long job. One by one we each had a bath and washed our bodies quickly. We were not allowed to soak in the bath, and I can't imagine what the water would have looked like by the time the last one got into it. We even had to dry ourselves using the same towel; I only hope Mum used our ages for what order we went into the bath. I would have been the second one and the water should have hopefully been fairly clean and the towel drier. I can't remember a lot of my very early days in Warren Street; I do know we were often left alone with Janet to oversee us, which seemed to be quite acceptable in those days. I think Mum use to get lonely without Dad and probably needed to have a break away from us all. Nan lived next door, so we could always go and get her if there were any problems. It was a big responsibility for Janet, one which, I may add, she took very seriously. In those days nearly everyone had a kitchenette (a large upright cupboard) in their kitchen; there was no such thing as a fitted kitchen. I can remember one day when Mum was out, I climbed onto the letdown of the kitchenette to get something from the top cupboard and the whole kitchenette fell on top of me. It was a miracle I wasn't badly injured. My sister was horrified checking I had not hurt myself, and telling me off at the same time. I was fine, just very scared about what Mum would say, as the kitchenette was broken and it didn't have a letdown any more. There was also a time when someone knocked on the front door and we all had to be quiet, but we knew the drill: stop talking and be prepared to hide behind the settee. We were quite use to this, as Mum often didn't want to answer the door in case it was the rent man or some other poor money collector. We had to hide behind the settee in case someone ventured into our backyard to look through the window. In this case, the knocking at the door was persistent, so Mum directed me to go to the door and tell him she wasn't home. I went to the door and said," Mum told me to tell you she is not here." You can imagine Mum's reaction, and boy, did I get into trouble for that slip-up. Mum had to face the rent man and tell him it was a mistake, giving all sorts of excuses. I should imagine Mum would have had second thoughts about me answering the front door in the future. There was no TV in those days, and we were subject to a strict routine so I would think we went to bed reasonably early or listened to the radio, I really can't remember. I do know Mum and Dad must have loved listening to music because I can remember word for word many songs from the 1950's and even before that. Usually, when you hear a song, you can recollect where or when you first heard it, but when I listen to music from the past, I just see Mum and Dad with no such recollection.

I'm so pleased we had such happy times in that house and memories we could call upon in later times of unhappiness. Life seemed to be so easy for us children, despite the complications regarding money, which at this stage we just didn't understand.

CHAPTER TWO

Mum and Dad

"In the happiest of our childhood memories, our parents were happy too"

Robert Brault

MY DAD WAS A FISHERMAN who sailed out of Fleetwood, and I know nothing of Mum and Dad's life together before I was born. I would have loved to have known how they met and how they felt about each other. I know they met during the war because their marriage certificate shows their service numbers, and they were married on Wednesday 01 November 1944. Dad was in the Royal Navy Patrol Service and stationed in Malta and Gibraltar at that time. Apparently, during the Second World War, there was a sudden increase in the number of weddings as people were unsure of what the future held, they were anxious to formalize their relationships, and were perhaps in need of some hope and joy, maybe this applied to Mum and Dad. Men and women overcame the obstacles of bombs and managed the rationing with ingenuity, on their way to the altar. Many married in Registry Offices, and often in uniform. The war was coming to a head in 1944, and my Mum and Dad did happen to get married in the Registry Office; Dad was twenty-three, and Mum was twenty. Sadly we have no photographs of their wedding, and I do wonder if they were in uniform. I can't remember my Mum ever talking about her wedding day, maybe she did and I just didn't listen, or I was too young to remember. If they married in Blackpool then they would have had to catch a tram or bus from Fleetwood, cars were for emergencies only and a wedding car was governed by distance, petrol consumed and a time limit of two hours, so I doubt they had this luxury. I also doubt they had a wedding reception because of rationing which was strictly controlled during the war, when everyone would have been feeling the pinch.

I think Mum and Dad may have met through their Fleetwood connection rather than their war service, as Mum was in the WAAF, and Dad was in the Royal Navy Reserve. Perhaps they met while on leave; I would have loved to know their story. There was a tale about Mum having to choose between a fellow in the RAF and my Dad, I'm not sure how true this was, but I know she picked the right man. I did find on the back of a WAAF group photo (which was signed just before Mum was going on leave to be married) a signature with the message "Still hoping," so he may have been the mystery man. Mum was called Kathleen Botham but was known as Kay and Bottom to many of her WAAF friends, and a lady called Teddy was her best friend. There is no doubt Mum loved her time in the WAAF, and I'm sure she would have had many tales to tell about her experience. I never saw my Mum with an engagement ring, so I don't think they got engaged, which is no real surprise. In those war years, many couples married quickly because they never knew if they would ever return home again. Mum would have needed her mother's permission to marry, and both Mum and Dad would have had to get special leave from their Officers in Charge. Mum's sister Vera was one of their witnesses, and the other was a man called G Fecitt, who must have been one of their friends as I don't recognize the name, maybe he was Dad's friend.

Dad was born on 03 June 1921, at 10 Victoria Street Fleetwood, he was the fifth and youngest child of Jim and Mary Gorst and he had four siblings. His dad worked for Fleetwood Corporation as a horseman and then later for the Parks Department. Dad lost his mum when he was seven, and he was brought up by his sisters Beatrice and Margaret. His older brother William Henry got lost overboard from a trawler in 1936 when he was twenty-three, so Dad had many times of sadness in his young life. Dad attended the Testimonial School, which was in Lord Street, and spent most of his young life during the Great Depression 1929-1939. The money would have been short for the family, and he wouldn't have had many if any, luxuries in his life. It must have been a tough time for him, especially after losing his mother in 1928. Those years were at a time of massive unemployment throughout Britain, with most families having to depend on welfare payments. Although Fleetwood's main industry was fishing, it would have no doubt, still felt the impact of those Great Depression years.

Dad joined the Royal Navy Reserve on the 12 June 1939 just nine days after his eighteenth birthday. During the Second World War, he was in the minesweepers as a Petty Officer, and he looked very handsome in his Navy uniform. During those war service years he was involved in frequent explosions. The potential for minesweepers to strike a mine was immense and he often ending up in the water, sometimes for many hours floating in debris and oil. He eventually had to take medicine for his stomach which was damaged due to swallowing that oil while he was in the water. He used to have bottles of a particular medicine and one of our jobs was to collect his medication from the chemist before he went to sea. The medicine came in large glass bottles filled with a white mixture. I can vaguely remember him collapsing one time when he was home from sea, we were living in Warren Street at that time. An ambulance arrived, and they took Dad to hospital with what I think was a perforated ulcer in his stomach. He was very ill, and if he had been at sea, he would have died.

The history of the Royal Naval Reserve is compelling, and my Dad would have had no compulsion about joining up. I imagine he would have thought it was exciting and the right thing to do, to be part of the war. I think he would have been a fisherman since leaving school probably from age fourteen, so he would already have had four years sea experience. Dad would have been very knowledgeable regarding navigation and the workings of trawlers and he was given wartime advancement at a young age. He was promoted to Leading Seaman and then Petty Officer. The Royal Naval Reserve related to people who earned their living by seafaring but would be available in case of hostilities. The service mobilized in August 1939, and Sparrow's Nest in Lowestoft became the Central Depot of the Royal Naval Patrol Service. Its location was at the most easterly point of Great Britain, and it was the closest British military establishment to the enemy. It was here that Dad was stationed throughout his war years. It was during WW1 when the advantages of using these small ships for minesweeping was recognized and these trawlers were known to be excellent seaworthy boats. The crews from the peacetime fishing fleets had been encouraged to join the Royal Naval Reserve, and many Fleetwood fishermen served on the minesweepers. The deployment of fishermen left a shortage of fish for the country, and Fleetwood dock was the temporary home to many trawlers from Hull and Grimsby. Within a short period, the Royal Navy had almost taken over Lowestoft with the establishment of no fewer than five Naval Bases. Dad's base was HMS Europa, which was the Royal Navy Patrol Service Headquarters. Combined vessels from the Royal Naval Patrol Service were on convoy duty in the Atlantic and the Arctic, in the Mediterranean and the Far East. Throughout the early years of the war, German mines were laid by sea and air in the waters around the British Isles in an attempt to stop the coastal convoys, which were used frequently to keep Britain supplied. It was the work of the Royal Navy Patrol Service to keep the shipping lane clear so that the convoys could continue, and this meant constant minesweeping, which is what Dad did. Unfortunately for Dad, many of the minesweepers he sailed in were blown up but miraculously he

survived. After clearing the area of mines, it was a simple task for E-Boats or aircraft to lay mines again, so it was a constant mission to keep these shipping lanes safe. (Royal Naval Patrol Service Association 2013 Internet)

Dad was mobilized very quickly in 1939, and in 1940 he was sailing on the *HMT St Achilleus* clearing mines around the Dunkirk area when it was blown up by a German mine. Many young sailors lost their lives, and Dad was in the water for many hours before being rescued. My

Dad in his Navy uniform

sister remembered Dad telling this story, but I had no memory of it. I often wondered when I got older, whether it was, in fact, an accurate account, not that I doubted my sister, but stories can get muddled over time. When I received my Dad's Navy records two years ago, the sinking of the minesweeper is documented and the fact that Dad had indeed been saved from the water. I was happy to tell Janet she had been correct and her memory of the event was accurate. One of the most exciting moments in the whole of my research, and there have been many, was to receive Dad's Naval record, which described him in 1939. It stated he had brown hair and brown eyes, a fresh complexion, and gave his height and chest measurements. I had forgotten how tall Dad was. He also had a scar on his left thigh, which is something I didn't know. I do wonder how he got that scar; maybe it was an accident at sea or from when he was a child. You may wonder why I was so excited by this information and why I would want to include it in my story, but the simple answer is I had never given those descriptive details any thought over the years. Dad's image in my mind had slipped away, relying only on black and white photographs to remember him by, and this new information made him very real to me. I did try hard to remember Dad in the years before 1959, but his fishing life took him away from home for long periods, and I think as a young child, you do not see those sorts of details. Dad was away two to three weeks at a time and only home for two to three days between, so is it any wonder my memories of him are few, except now, I will never forget those brown eyes.

Dad had a ceremonial sword and war medals which we often got out of the cupboard to admire. Dad was proud of his uniform and the ceremonial sword was his treasure. Regrettably both those items are no longer in the family and they could have been our treasures to keep forever. Dad's medals were given to my younger brother but sadly went missing after Harry died, and I believe his sword got broken by Dad's nephew (uncle Ken's son) many years ago. My sister did obtain replacement medals, but unfortunately, they don't have his service number on them as the originals would have had. I am so proud of my Dad and all he achieved while in the Navy, he strove to be the best he could. Even during the fifties, when we were all so young, he managed to continue training and attained the rank of Lieutenant. The Royal Navy documented his death in their obituary list, and I'm not sure even Mum knew that. I would like to think that any of my family attending the Remembrance Day Service will remember my Dad for his duty and bravery in World War 2.

Mum was born on 02 January 1924 at 86 Warren Street and was the third child of Jennie and Jack Botham. Her father was also a fisherman who had died two years before she was married. I think Mum would have had a happy childhood, my Nan was such a loving, gentle, hardworking woman and they remained a very close family all their lives. Mum was close to her sisters, although I'm sure there were times when they got frustrated at the way she managed her money. They loved her, but at the end of the day, they were not walking in her shoes.

There are so many gaps to Mum's young life, but I do know she was in the WAAF (Women's Auxiliary Air Force). The WAAF was established in June 1939 by King George VI for duty with the Royal Air Force (RAF) in time of war. The WAAF at that time was not an independent organization, nor was it wholly integrated within the RAF. Instead, it was interlinked with its 'parent' force to substitute, where possible, women for RAF personnel. It was mobilized on 28 August 1939, and within the year, tens of thousands of women had volunteered to serve. In 1941 the WAAF became part of the Armed Forces of the Crown, subject to the Air Force Act, its members greeted this with pride and enthusiasm. With conscription for women introduced from December 1941, the ranks swelled further so that by July 1943 the peak strength was 182,000. In 1945 250 thousand women had served in the WAAF in over 110 different trades, supporting operations around the world. They were an integral and vital part of the Royal Air Force's war effort. (Wikipedia)

Mum when she was about 19 in her WAAF uniform

Mum was very proud of her time in the WAAF, and like Dad was only eighteen when she joined up. She talked fondly about the people she met while stationed at Market Drayton in Shropshire. Her job was driving Government vehicles ranging from ambulances to supply vehicles. This included driving the aircraft crews to their planes on the airstrips and other duties. I'm sure she would have taken many pilots to their planes and I wonder how many returned. Although she learned to drive while serving in the WAAF, she never got her civilian license, and there are many stories to be told about that. Mum was an excellent driver and loved to drive, she taught my husband to drive many years later, and she was also a taxi driver in Fleetwood for a short time. It sounds like Mum did some things which she wasn't always allowed to do while stationed in Shropshire. A story Aunty Myra told me was that she would arrive home suddenly to Fleetwood quite unexpectedly, without letting anyone know. These surprise trips mostly happened when her Dad was in from sea. Mum loved her father, and Aunty Myra told me they had a very close bond. None of the family ever knew if she had permission to drive to Fleetwood, but they were always excited to see her. Mum would not think she was doing anything wrong and would have managed to talk her way out of any situation. I could just imagine her turning up and surprising the family because she was such a social person and loved to be with everyone. Mum also had to have her appendix removed while she was in Market Drayton, and all the family went to visit her, which would have been quite an arduous journey in those war years. I wonder how they travelled the 102-mile trip and what it cost for all the family. It would have been a significant undertaking financially during those war years, but it did not stop the whole family from wanting to see her. There was a railway station in Fleetwood at that time, so I presume they would have travelled by rail. It would have been a long journey with having to change stations along the way. The railway station in Fleetwood was a magnificent building, it was well maintained and was known as a terminal station. Unfortunately, it was closed in 1966 and two years later totally demolished. The Beeching cuts in the mid 1960's was responsible for this action which left many Fleetwood people angry and sad at its loss. I am so proud of my Mum and Dad, serving in the war and having a commitment to duty at such a young age. My Dad, in particular, risked his life like so many did during the war. He was lucky to have survived, and we were very fortunate to have had some precious years with him.

I think Mum would have been a pioneer in her time; she loved to do things that were exciting and was not afraid to take on a challenge. There was a discussion at one time about us all going to live in Borneo when

Dad got a chance to serve there. We use to talk excitedly about living in a foreign country, not understanding the implications of this. However, we didn't live that dream, and I'm not sure why we didn't go, but I think my mother, the explorer, would have been disappointed. There was also talk of us going to live in Australia, and we talked excitedly about riding to school on horseback and living in perpetual hot weather, but this also didn't happen. It must have been Mum's influence that sparked the idea of emigration in my head, although I think I was a bit more realistic as I never planned to do anything on horseback! I can now see she wanted us to have a better life and for Dad to leave the sea, something I also wanted for my husband and children many years later.

Mum and Dad circa 1944

Mum and Dad certainly made a handsome couple, and I know they loved each other. I can only remember one argument they had, and it was while we lived in Wingrove Road. I have no idea what it was about but can remember being frightened by it, as they very seldom argued. Mum tried to make sure everything was ready for those precious few days when Dad was in from sea. There was always chicken on the table, which was a luxury for most households, and the house was clean and tidy, (usually down to Janet's hard work). It is sad to think Mum and Dad had only fifteen years together, and much of that time was spent apart while Dad was at sea. But I do know they were happy and loved each other.

I really hated Dad going to sea and I always said I would never marry a fisherman because I would want him home by my side, how naïve I was then, there were no other option when you lived in Fleetwood. It was inevitable that I should fall in love with a fisherman and start to experience the same life Mum had experienced. Our town breathed the fishing industry. The grocery shops supplied trawlers, and engineers maintained their engines, braiders made and mended the nets, lumpers landed the fish, and the fish merchants bought the fish. The pubs were popular and supplied the much-needed entertainment to replenish the souls of many young men to make the dangerous trip to the sea again. I would say that when I was younger, every person in Fleetwood was linked to the sea or had a relative who went sea. The connection between many fishing families is historically enduring, bringing a closeness which still exists, but is sadly getting weaker as the years move on.

CHAPTER THREE

The Early Years

"I've never tried to block out the memories of the past, even though some are painful. I don't understand people who hide from their past. Everything you live through helps to make you the person you are now"

Sophia Loren

WHEN I WAS BORN, THE National Health Service was being developed and began on 5 July 1948, and I cannot imagine what it would have been like for families before then. The railways were nationalized on 01 January to become British Railways, and times were changing in that post-war era. Although they had ration books, people were trying to make the best of what they had, and there was an air of joyous anticipation for the future. The war had taken its toll on the lives of many families, with many of their loved ones killed. Families were split up their children sent away to the country to protect them from the falling bombs. But they had survived the terrible war. I remember people talking fondly about the war, saying they were good times when people cared for their neighbours and friends, they stuck together, and they had no other option but to help each other. Time was doing its job of healing like time always does.

I have a feeling the Government tried to do its best for the country in those days. There were no benefits like today, and Mums only income apart from Dad's wage was the family allowance which she received each week. I can remember that family allowance book so well, it was often a godsend for many families. The Post Office managed the payments and the more children you had, the more money you received. It is interesting to know how this payment developed as I believe it was opposed by many who thought the men who earned a living should maintain their children out of their own wage.

A White Paper of Family Allowances was published in May 1942 giving costs for various levels of family allowance. These were not immediately adopted, and following the publication of the Beveridge Report, which called for subsistence levels of payments to be uprated with the cost of living, the Family Allowances Act 1945 was passed. The allowance provided a five-shilling per week payment for each child, after the first one, and was there to support large families. It was set well below the nine shillings a week subsistence level (further devalued by inflation) recommended by Beveridge. In 1952 the rate was increased to eight shillings per week and in 1956 the price for the third and subsequent children was increased to ten shillings per week. The maximum age for payments for dependent children increased from fifteen to eighteen at that time. (Wikipedia)

Mum's family allowance book had its value, not just in the weekly payments which it provided, but it was a tool to borrow money. If Mum had no money left on a Tuesday, then she would ask family or friends to loan her the family allowance that was due on Friday. Whoever that guardian angel was would sign the book alongside Mum's signature of authorization at the front. That kind person would then collect the money owed on Friday and return the book to Mum, waiting for its next mission to begin. I know Mum was not alone in this practice. I believe a lot of families had to undertake this financial arrangement. The trouble with Mum was she often signed her family allowance away for a few weeks if she needed a more substantial sum of money, which often left her in debt. I'm not sure if my Dad was aware of the things Mum did for cash such as pawning his best suit when he went to sea or borrowing money from my Nan or aunties. If he did, I presume he thought she needed to do whatever it took to manage and get us fed.

We lived next door to my Nan and our aunties, who were very much involved in our lives, often putting food on the table in times of hardship.

Hardships were often, Dad being a fisherman relied on a good trip to pay bills and buy us what we needed, if he had a bad trip, he could have ended up owing money to the fishing firm. "How could that happen," one might ask, but Dad's income was not guaranteed because the fishermen had to sign onto a ship as casuals. Despite these hardships, Mum and Dad tried their very best to give us treats, keep us well dressed, and have happy times together.

Every Whitsun, we got a new outfit, and Mum and Dad often purchased our clothes from a shop on the corner of the street where we lived called Children's Corner. It was a lovely shop, but the clothes were more expensive, and I certainly felt quite posh wearing them. I can remember many of the outfits I wore from my younger days, and the few photos we have as youngsters show us all wearing decent clothes. Dad made his homecomings special, and if he made a good trip, we would go to Blackpool and go up Blackpool Tower, play on the arcades, and eat at a popular café called the Lobster Pot, frequented by many fishermen and their families when times were right. The Isle of Man boat sailed from Fleetwood, and once Dad bought tickets for us all to go. It was a popular excursion with hundreds of people queuing to get on the boat. It must have cost Dad a fortune to take us all, not only in the price of the tickets but also in getting around the island and dining out in cafes. We went to one café and I ordered chips but when they arrived, they were crinkly. I had never seen crinkly chips before, and from that day on I believed you could only get them in the Isle of Man. My Dad was a stickler for good manners which stays with me to this day, we always had to say please and thank you, respect our elders and never answer back. We were also not allowed to make chip butties if we were eating out. I loved chip butties, so I devised a plan to satisfy my needs in this regard. I would take a bite of my bread, then pretend to chew and swallow it, then I would put a chip into my mouth and eat the chip and bread together, problem solved. Dad didn't seem to notice, and I thought myself quite smart to fool him, or did I? How I would have loved to talk to him about the antics we all got up to, I'm sure he would have loved all the chatter with his family.

At Easter, we got chocolate Easter eggs from all of our family, and we use to place them in our front window on display, like trophies we had won. It was fun to walk down the street and count how many Easter eggs were in the windows of other homes, and with great pride, we usually had the most, of course, with six children we would. One of our traditions was, we didn't eat them till Easter Monday after we had been to the Mount to roll them down the hill (along with most of the kids from Fleetwood). Rolling the Easter egg was to signify moving the stone off the entrance to the cave where they put Jesus after his crucifixion. This biblical event took place on the third day (Easter Monday) when resurrected. We were not a religious family, but it was what everyone else did, and I must add (for my Australian friends) that there was not an Easter Bunny in sight! Easter certainly was a fun time for us, and apart from eating chocolate for breakfast, lunch, and dinner, we got to make Easter baskets at school filled with small chocolate Easter eggs. We also sang hymns in assembly such as "There is a Green Hill Far Away" which depicted the crucifixion of Jesus. I use to love singing hymns much to the annoyance of my brothers and sisters, who always tried to bundle me to the under stairs cupboard so they couldn't hear me. I love singing hymns to this day, but of course now my voice is croaky and I would deserve to be put in the under stairs cupboard now.

I attended Sunday school at times and did Religious studies at school, which I enjoyed. I am not particularly religious, but events from my childhood and even to some extent life now still follow aspects of my childhood. Being Christened was essential to most people when I was younger, and I note to this day, the practice is as widespread today in Fleetwood as it was then. When I was researching my family tree, I gleaned a lot of information from the Parish records regarding my ancestors because they were all baptized. I think this is why I am such a traditionalist. My childhood was routine and welcomed; we did the same events each year, but they were safe and enjoyed by us all. When you speak with Fleetwood people from my era about our childhood, they can identify exactly with those same traditions as most children did the same things we did.

There were three classes of people in Fleetwood when I was younger; those that were well off, those that had a little and those that had nothing. I remember hovering between the ones that had a bit but often skirted around the edges of those that had nothing. I am not ashamed of the fact that we were quite poor because Mum tried to give us a good life, and most of the time, she was successful. There were a few Government initiatives that helped, especially when we were very young such as free concentrated orange juice which was the best orange juice I have ever tasted. The Government also gave free concentrated Vitamin B drops, which tasted quite nice and the dreaded cod liver oil, which tasted terrible. We had to have a dose of these vitamins every day. There were also free tins of baby food called National Dried milk powder, which I am sure would have been welcomed by those mothers finding it hard to feed their families. We never went without food in the early days, but as we got older, the days when we worried where the next meal was coming from seemed to get closer together. The days in Warren Street, however, were my happiest days; we spent the summers on the beach and the winters by the fire listening to the radio, playing cards, and playing together with our toys. The advantages of having a large family was that we all played well together, and school was one of our favourites. We took turns at being the teacher sitting at our makeshift desks doing reading and writing and being told off by the teacher which was the central theme. That fact may have been why we fought to be the teacher, to be the boss. We also had a post office set each, where we learned to write our letters, and put the stamp on the envelope correctly, making sure the Queen's head was not placed upside down. Letter writing was quite formal in those days, which is not so relevant today.

We all loved to read our annuals which were usually bought for us at Christmas. The annuals ranged from Dandy and Beano to annuals of film stars. Somehow Virginia Mayo sticks in my mind, and I'm not sure why. I probably thought she was beautiful and I would have liked to be her when I grew up, who knows? We were also proud owners of a dolls Silver Cross pram, which must have cost Mum and Dad a fortune with having to buy three. Each one was complete with a lifesize doll and a beautiful cover set. Janet had a twin pram, but unfortunately, it got stolen not long after she got it, and we never saw it again. I have many happy memories of when we were all together; when tragedy was hiding; waiting to pounce. We were a happy bunch, and when I see photographs of us together, I smile because at least one of us is making a funny face, but most of all we looked happy. Mum use to tune in to a particular radio band where the skippers could talk on-air. We all looked forward to this time and would all huddle around the radio, hoping to hear Dad talk. We would all be very excited to listen to his voice, especially if he mentioned our particular name; which he always tried to do. Dad would give Mum an idea when he would be home, and he usually asked, were we all being good kids. We were never sure how it worked; it seemed like a marvel to us. I should imagine Mum, like us, was happy to hear his voice and know he was safe at that moment.

The fishermen of Fleetwood had tough lives, trying to make a living out of such an unpredictable industry. These brave men had to buy the specialist clothes they needed to carry out their work, such as heavy-duty socks, wet weather gear, gloves, boots, and even a knife to gut the fish they caught. A small wage was available to the wives each week, but Mum's wages were never enough to last her the week. That is why she was always trying to borrow money; it must have been a nightmare for her. One of the many things she did for money was to pawn my Dad's one and only suit. I'm sure the pawnshop was as popular with other families as it was with ours. If you wanted to buy anything from the pawnshop, you went to the front entrance in St Peter's Place, but if you tried to pawn anything, you went to the back entrance. Fortunately for Mum, the back entrance just happened to be in our back alley. Many families had to resort to pawning their belongings even though there was great shame attached to using the pawnshop. As soon as we waved Dad's ship away, my sister or I would take the indispensable suit to the pawnshop where it would be wrapped in brown paper and assigned a number. The man would give us a ticket and a small amount of money. I can't remember how much, but I don't think it was a lot. The treasured brown parcel would then be put on a shelf, not knowing its importance in providing six children with a few meals. As soon as Mum knew Dad was due in from sea, we would be given money (often borrowed again) and sent to the pawnshop to buy Dad's best suit back. The suit was then taken to the Fleet cleaners and returned on a coat hanger covered with plastic as if it had never been on a mercy mission. I'm sure the pawnshop owner would never have sold the suit, and I don't know what Mum would have done if he had, but I shudder at this thought as it was Dad's only suit.

Once I was older and had my own family, I was able to reflect with understanding how hard life would have been for my Mum and Dad and how worried they must have been when they had no money. We were all born quite quickly after each other as there would have been no birth control like today. It was not unusual to have large families in those days, so we were all in the same boat as many families were. It did not help that Mum was not great with money, not that I'm blaming Mum; it's just the truth. Mum was young and had the challenge of six children to feed, clothe and look after. The part my Nan and aunties played in our lives was pivotal to our upbringing, and I can't say enough about how vital our extended family was. They often made the difference to us eating a decent meal or in some circumstances, no meal at all. Our aunties taught us how to bake, how to share, and how to love unconditionally, and I don't know how we would have managed without them. I should imagine Mum would have been so grateful to them, and they remained very close till each one sadly passed away.

Aunty Vera, Mum holding Harry, Aunty Myra and Aunty Gladys

CHAPTER FOUR

Brothers and Sisters

"The relationship with our brothers and sisters is one of the most important in our lives. Although it can sometimes be complex, the sibling bond is one of the most enduring"

Author unknown

JANET WAS THE FIRST OF my siblings to arrive and, as the eldest, had a considerable part to play in our upbringing. Jan was sometimes the anchor to the family while we were growing up and Mum relied on her to take care of the younger members of the family. Jan had to run the house from a very early age, which she did to the best of her ability, and with a happy disposition most of the time. I'm sorry to say in contrast, my temperament was nothing like Janet's as I always tried to sidestep any responsibility. I grumbled most of the time if I had to do any cooking and cleaning and I'm sure at times I got away with it because Mum would be tired of me arguing.

Jan wanted to be a nurse at a very early age, and she became a Cadet Nurse shortly after leaving school. Sadly, she had to abandon her career when she married George as Cadet Nurses were not allowed to marry in those days. Instead Jan chose George, the love of her life and they had many happy years together. I know Jan never regretted leaving nursing at that time, she was only seventeen when she got married in 1963 but her marriage never faulted. Jan had so much practise looking after us all and taking charge of the house that she would have been the most experienced newlywed you could find. I'm pleased to say Jan did eventually become a Registered Nurse, which she was quite rightly so proud of achieving. It took a lot of hard work and determination for her to go back to College, juggling work and her two children to realize that qualification. Jan grew up just knowing how to care for people, and there have been many people in Fleetwood who have been the recipients of her care while she was a theatre nurse at Fleetwood Hospital. George adored Janet, and they had a happy life together, enjoying many overseas trips to New Zealand and Australia to visit us. Sadly, George died in 1999 from cancer, a loss that devastated the family. For Dave and I, we not only lost a brother in law but a dear friend. I am still very close to my sister, and we have spent many happy times together as adults, something I will never forget.

Patricia Elizabeth was born on 22 June 1949, and she was such a pretty little girl with blonde hair and the sweetest face. Now Mum had three girls to look after. We were all great friends as we grew up, spending many happy hours playing together. Mum chose to dress Trisha and me in the same clothes when we were tiny but thankfully did not continue the practice as we got older, we were quite different in that regard. As teenagers, we had different friends as one would expect, so we never really hung out together. I don't think she joined the youth club, which I went to, but I may be wrong about that. We had a different set of friends, so I am not surprised we each did our own thing. Trish loved my Mum, and they were very close; looking back, I think they were good friends as well as mother and daughter. I know Trish was devastated when Mum died. Mum let Trisha smoke with her from a very young age which had a sad and devastating outcome in the end but in fairness to Mum, I don't think the message about smoking in those days, was as strong as it is today. Unfortunately, with my move to New Zealand, I lost touch with Trish and relied on Mum to update me on events regarding Trish's family. It was difficult to communicate as letter writing was the only form of correspondence. There was no internet, and the cost of an international phone call was out of reach for many, including me. Trish and John had five children together who I have spasmodically watched grow up into lovely adults, all doing well while holding their Mum's memory close to their hearts. How proud of them she would be, and how loved they were by her. We were always happy to see each other when I visited Fleetwood, and our relationship would just take up as if I had never been away. It was hard in those days to maintain any meaningful relationships, especially when bringing up families of our own. On one of my visits to Fleetwood Trish and I had a fall-out, but thank goodness we made up, and we felt quite close to each other in the end. Unfortunately, this was the last time I had with Tricia, as she died of lung cancer in 2002. She was far too young to die, and it was another devastating loss for the family, especially her husband and children.

James Roger was born on 26 September 1950. I think Mum and Dad would have rejoiced at having a baby boy in their lives after having three girls. Jimmy, as we called him in his younger days, was a lovely little boy who we all adored. He was looked after by us all, and even I loved taking care of him. How could we not, he had such a gentle nature which stayed with him all his life. Jim was a hard worker who was always in employment, and people thought highly of him. I wish I had asked him what it was like to have three adoring sisters around when growing up; why didn't I ask? I'm sure Jimmy would have enjoyed attention when he was younger, but as he got older, attention was something he wouldn't have liked. In the early days Jimmy often stayed with me, keeping me company while Dave was at sea. I appreciated his company and the girls loved their Uncle Jimmy. He would often babysit for us and would look after the girls for hours and play games with them. I think he liked the fact that I was quite organized and the house was always tidy with food in the cupboard. I can hear you all saying "wow she must have changed," and I had. I had the responsibility of my own house and children now, something I relished and enjoyed.

I think Jim and I maintained our level of closeness even though I lived overseas. It was not in the way of communication, but I always felt that bond when we were together. I like to think that anyway. Jim went to work in Scotland for a while where he met his wife Rita, who eventually came to live at my Mum's house in Heathfield Road. Mum enjoyed having Rita there, and they got on well together. Mum liked the company and Rita was quite comical; they seemed to be on the same wavelength. We were fortunate to be visiting Fleetwood when their first daughter was born, and I just loved her right from the start. I would babysit her at any opportunity and often looked after her overnight at my Nan's house, where we were staying.

Jim had been very unwell for a long time, mainly due to the death of our brother Harry which hit him hard. He was devastated as they were close brothers, and he never really got over it. Jim was so brave and courageous, fighting one battle after another with no complaints. He had the strength that not many of us would be able to find. Jim had been critically ill, and he struggled to win that battle only to face another, which eventually took his life. I was devastated when I got the call to come home in 2009 because Jim was dying of cancer. I wanted to get back and see him, but I knew he would know he was dying if he saw me. Jim had told me on one of our telephone calls that while he was critically ill in the hospital the first time, he hadn't wanted me to come home because it would have sent a sign he was dying. This left me in a dilemma as I didn't want to be the bearer of this news, but I had to see him as I knew it would be the last time. It was a long flight home from Australia, and I was worried I wouldn't make it in time. My sisters met me at the airport, and on the drive to Jim's house, I asked if Jim knew he was dying and they told me that he did know. Sadly, his first words when he saw me was, "I'm dying," and my heart shattered as it was the very words I didn't wanted to hear. I knew he would say them though, and I could only answer quietly, "I know love." I respected him too much to lie and loved him too much to deny him those words. I'm not sure the family understood that moment, but Jim and I did, and those words broke my heart. His funeral was both fantastic and sad. There were so many people at the church who thought a lot of Jim, friends and family both showing their respect. How loved he was and how we would all sadly miss him.

Margaret Anne was born on 30 January 1952, and I can't remember her very earlier days. What I can remember is her lovely smile and a willingness to participate in everything we did. Marg loved her family, and I think where she sat in the pecking order had a lot to do with this. Having older sisters and an older brother meant she was included in all we did. Mum would insist we take the younger siblings out with us, and we spent many happy hours down on the beach, making sandcastles and paddling in the water. A favourite was digging out the sand near the water's edge to build a boat and then waiting for the tide to come in and surround the sand boat with water. We did have a lot of fun together, we had to stick together as Jan, (mainly Jan) and I had to look after our brothers and sisters, and we did. Marg adored Harry when he was born, and her mothering instincts took over with her protectiveness towards him. It is of no wonder that she still, to this day, looks out for everyone with caring messages if she thinks someone or something is not right with the family. Marg joined the sea cadets' band when she was a teenager and played the bass drum, which she was extremely good at, and it suited her. They played at the Edinburgh Tattoo and at Earls Court, which were both highlights for Marg. In 1970 Marg emigrated to New Zealand, and it was good to have a family member with us, especially for the children who loved their Aunty Marg. She settled in well and worked in the kitchens of the hospital where I worked. They liked her, as she was a hard worker and a good friend to many of them. Marg eventually married and had a child, but sadly the marriage didn't work out, so Marg returned to England. It was fortunate that she went home when she did as she was able to spend some happy times with Mum before she died.

William Henry (Harry), the youngest family member, was born on 01 February 1957, and Trudy, my daughter, shares his birthdate. We were all in raptures over him when he was born. He was just so cute, and none of us minded looking after him. I remember with horror the day Harry was badly scalded and almost died. We lived in Wingrove Road, and the house was always busy. Jan was in the kitchen and had made a pot of tea. The scalding hot tea was sat on the grill let-down of the cooker and Harry, who was only about 18-month-old, toddled into the kitchen straight towards the teapot. Somehow the scalding hot tea spilt all over his head and on the top of his body. Mum screamed for Janet and me to run to the telephone box and call for an ambulance. The phone box was quite a way away, and I don't think we had ever ran that fast in our lives. The ambulance had already arrived before we got back, and by that time, Mum had taken all Harry's clothes off and wrapped him in a cotton sheet. The doctor at the hospital praised Mum for saving Harry's life as getting those clothes off him was the best thing she could have done. It must have been terrifying for him, the pain he endured would have been severe. We all cried when he was taken away in the ambulance and although we knew it was serious, we didn't know how serious it was. He spent three months in our hospital at Fleetwood, and we all missed him so much. In those days, children were not allowed to visit anyone in the hospital, and we were worried he would miss us or even forget us. He had a lot of attention from the nurses, and other patients so was quite happy without us. It was hard though, as we all missed him so much. When he was better, the nurses started to put his cot outside for fresh air, but I think it was an arrangement Mum had made with them so we could see him. On bright sunny days, we would go to the hospital and peer through the hedge to see if he was outside. If he was there, we would call his name and attract his attention, while jostling to get a good view of him. The first time this happened, it was like looking at a little dark boy as his gorgeous little face had been so burnt, but this eventually faded, and all that was left to remind us of his accident were scars to both of his shoulders. It must have been a strange feeling for Harry when he came out of the hospital because he had received constant attention and was never left alone. He would start to cry at bedtime and I felt sorry for him, so I volunteered to lie with him till he went asleep. One of the things that calmed Harry was to have his shoulders gently massaged until he fell asleep. I did this every single night until the long summer evenings, and playing out with my friends, seemed to be far more important. When I thought he was asleep and I tried to sneak out of the bedroom, Harry would cry. Mum had no sympathy and reminded me that I had started it, and I would just have to get on with it. When we got older, I told Harry on many occasions about the great sacrifice I made for him and he just use to laugh. Harry followed in Dad's footsteps and went to sea on the trawlers. He became a young skipper and quite a successful one, but unfortunately, we were to suffer yet another tragedy. Harry died in Fleetwood from a terrible accident in 1986. At this stage Harry had been fishing out of Lowestoft and on this occasion, he had brought the trawler to Fleetwood. He was boarding his boat when it was dark, and he must have lost his footing, falling into the dock. His body was found twenty-four hours later by the police divers. Harry was identified by my brother Jim, and it was to have a devastating effect on him for the rest of his life. I was in New Zealand at that time and when I received the phone call to tell me I just couldn't believe he was dead. Another loss for our family and such devastating news. I was a long away from my family, and I felt helpless, I just wanted to be home with them. I managed to get a flight back to England later that night. It was a long lonely journey on my own, with flashback memories of my little brother on my mind. Because he had moved to Lowestoft a few years before, it was where his funeral took place. It was a sombre funeral and attended by friends and shipmates many travelling from Fleetwood to attend. The wreaths and flowers were beautiful; there were anchors, ships, wheels, hearts, and messages. He had left behind five beautiful children; the youngest, also called Harry, was only two years old. It was like history repeating itself as my Dad had left six children, the youngest being age two, which of course, was Harry, and both had drowned. Harry's children are now all grown up with families of their own, and Harry would have loved his grandchildren. Although I can remember him jokingly, telling my girls not to call him Uncle as he was too young. We didn't see much of Harry's children after he died, and I have never understood why. We all made an effort to keep in touch, and I know Jan used to send cards and money to the children for their birthdays. I wrote letters regularly from New Zealand, but they were never acknowledged; I often wonder what Harry would have thought about this. The family had always been important to him and he would have been disappointed we were not part of his children's lives. It was wonderful, however, to see young Harry, Sarah-Jane and Michelle when Jim died, and I am so grateful they took the time to say goodbye to their Uncle Jim.

One thing I know about my siblings is that we loved each other and enjoyed happy times together. Our family grew up over the years, with three periods linked to our lives, these periods repeated over and over. Waiting with joy and excitement for Dad to come in from sea, enjoying every minute with him when he was home, then saying goodbye to him with a sadness in our hearts, knowing we might never see him again. Those periods continued for me until 1969 with my own husband Dave, a fisherman. That was until we hatched a plan that would change our lives forever, an idea, which I now see, was perhaps planted in my head by Mum when I was a young girl.

What a happy bunch we were

CHAPTER FIVE

My Nan

"What children need most are the essentials that grandparents provide in abundance. They give unconditional love, kindness, patience, humour, comfort, lessons in life, and, most importantly, cookies"

Rudy Giuliani

MY NAN WAS THE LOVELIEST gentlest person you could ever meet, and she was the centre of our world. We were so lucky to be living next door, which allowed us to spend lots of time with her, while she taught us many things. She made the best fried-bread and hot cocoa, which I loved, and nothing was too much trouble for her. Something is comforting and pleasurable about memories, even today, looking at cocoa takes me back to Nan and her instructions on how to make a cup of hot cocoa, I can also smell and taste it. That's what I love about memories. We would sit around in the evenings listening to the radio, and sometimes as a treat, she would give me 6d to get some chips or scraps from the chip shop, which was just around the corner. We always took turns to have an evening with Nan, and I realise now it was probably a chance to have one-on-ones with her, where we got to share her constant attention with us. How lucky we were, thank you, Nan.

Nan often had boarders staying at the house, and I guess it was a way to get some extra money, but it did mean Nan worked very hard. I'm not quite sure where everyone slept as it was only a three-bedroomed house, but she fitted them all in somewhere. The front bedroom was the biggest with two double beds, and I sometimes slept with Nan and Aunty Glad in there. I also stayed with Aunty Myra in the smallest bedroom as she was too scared to sleep on her own when Uncle Bob was at sea. There had been some unusual paranormal events happening in Nan's house that scared the whole family, but that is another story. The toilet was outside, so a potty was kept under the bed to wee in, I can almost hear you all saying yuk. Nearly every household had one, though, and it was better than walking down to the back of the yard in the cold weather. We did this until the houses got modernised, but of course, putting a bathroom upstairs meant losing a bedroom, so I think there would have been no hurry for Mum to do this. One thing I liked about Nan's house was that it was clean, and Nan had a regular cleaning routine that I loved. Washing was done Mondays in a big copper tub, which had to be heated up, and an old mangle was used to squeeze the water out of the clothes. It took all day to do the washing, which is a far cry from today's automated washing machines. Nan's boiler was copper and kept in the kitchen, and the mangle was kept in the old coal shed down the yard at the back of the house. The washing, especially the sheets were very heavy when they were wet, and there was only a wooden pair of tongs to get them out of the boiling hot water. The Dolly Tub was kept in the yard, and Nan had to carry buckets of water from the boiler to fill it. The clothes were washed, rubbing them across a corrugated board called a washing board. You sometimes see the old skittle bands playing a washing board using a thimble on their fingers. It was burdensome work for Nan, so little wonder that washing day was an all-day event, you certainly didn't need the gym for a workout! There was also a drying rack that hung from the living room ceiling, and Nan's rack always had perfectly ironed clothes airing on it. The early fire was an old stove with two ovens heated from the fire, and Nan could bake bread and biscuits in those ovens. Nan's house was warm and felt inviting; without a doubt, there would always be a kettle of water on the fireplace ready to make a cup of tea at any time. Nan welcomed visitors to the house, and they didn't need an invitation, there would be a knock on the door, Nan's name called out, and then in would walk the visitor, which is quite different today. Married women usually stayed home, so there was always somewhere to go for a cup of tea, making the community quite close and friendly. The oven had many purposes; even the cat's kittens were kept in it to keep warm (with the door open, of course). I remember Aunty Vera putting a tin of poultice in the oven to heat up, leaving the lid on, but unfortunately when she took the lid off, it blew up in her face, which must have been very painful for her.

The cellar was a scary place and accessed by stairs off the kitchen. It was a place where you could store old furniture and where the coal was stored. The coalman delivered the coal in sacks and dropped them through the grid into the cellar. The grid cover was located at the front of the house and had to be scrubbed clean after delivery. The coalman in those early days drove a horse and cart, later they were promoted to a truck which must have made their lives a lot easier, but they still had to sling the sacks on to their backs to carry them to the grid. Having to carry up a bucket of coal from the cellar was scary as there were no lights down there. The electricity meter was also kept down in the cellar and it had to be fed with money to keep the electricity running. None of us liked to go down there on our own, and if it were my turn, I would run up the steps sure a ghost was after me.

Every month or so, the meter reader would come and empty the meter, and sometimes you would get a rebate which was the difference between money put into the meter and the actual cost of the electricity. This rebate didn't happen to us very often as my Mum used to rub pennies on a stone to make the edges thinner, which tricked the meter into accepting them as shillings. Many families did this, and although it was illegal and frowned upon, the meter reader never said anything as I know he would have understood many families had to do it. Another way in which we survived. There were many times we had no electricity, and the house was in darkness. Somehow though, we had a good fire to sit in front of, and maybe Mum had to decide between the two, keeping us warm or having light. We had some lovely times in front of the fire, making up stories about the images we saw in the hot embers and flames. Looking back, I think of those times as being precious moments with all the family together, telling our stories and comforted by the light from the fire. In reality, when the house was in darkness, the young ones wouldn't go to the toilet on their own, scared the bogey man would get them, and when we left the heat of the fire, the house was freezing. We would have to climb into a cold bed, finding our way with help off the street light, that shined through the window. The front of Nan's house was immaculate, and she scrubbed the front doorstep with a donkey stone. Nearly everyone washed their steps this way, and I think it was a matter of pride to have a clean step and foyer. Nan would have been proud of her house, and she worked hard to maintain its cleanliness.

Our foyer and that of Nan's had beautiful tiles on the floor which you would pay a fortune for today, and I often wonder if the present owners kept them as both of those houses have now been modernised and don't look the same at all. Talking about the front step reminds me of a time, I was locked out of our house on one summer's night. We were all in bed, and the house was quiet, I sneaked downstairs to to tell Mum I couldn't sleep, but Mum wasn't there. I decided to go next door to Nan's as I thought that must be where she was, but Nan's front door was closed, I knocked, but no one answered. I decided the best course of action was to go back to bed, but to my horror, our front door had closed behind me, and I was left to sit on the doorstep for a few hours feeling forlorn; but not frightened. It was dark by the time I saw Mum walking down the street carrying a plastic bag in her hand and a goldfish swimming around in it. They had all been to the annual summer fairground which came to the park each year. Mum was horrified I had been on the doorstep on my own for a few hours. I would only have been about eight at the time, maybe even younger but it didn't seem to be a big deal, Mum didn't seem to be that worried. I think deep inside; she would have been worried as I got a telling off for getting out of bed in the first place. After all, Mum thought we were all safe and tucked up in bed asleep, not sat on the doorstep alone and in the dark.

When I started to research Nan's life, I was upset to discover her upbringing had been anything but happy. Nan's father didn't seem to care for her, and her mother, Jane tried to do the best she could. Nan was born in Flintshire, North Wales, and her father was a blacksmith. He was also a drinker who threw her and her mother Jane out of the house on many occasions. Poor Nan moved in and out of the workhouse because they had nowhere else to go, and Aunty Myra remembers Nan saying her childhood was sad. I don't think Nan ever talked about this, and I am so relieved she met my granddad and had what looks like, a very happy life with him. They had four girls together who they adored. I visited Wales on my last visit to the UK and took Aunty Myra to see the house where Nan lived when she was first married. I also went to the local archives to see if I could find the workhouse or school records. Unfortunately, I couldn't find Nan's admissions as the files for that particular workhouse was destroyed in a fire. Maybe it was meant for me not to see those admissions as the workhouse records were depressing to read, and I felt so sad. In some ways, I was relieved that I was not going to see Nan's name as I didn't want to find anything other than Nan was clean and not unkempt, that she was healthy and not sickly and that she was safe and not separated from her mother.

I am sad to say I lost real touch with my Nan following our move to New Zealand. When we returned in 1981, Nan was showing signs of dementia, and although I think she knew who I was, she didn't know me as an adult with children of my own. We stayed in Warren Street for a while as Nan wasn't living there at the time. I was always a bit scared in her house, especially when I had to go upstairs, and the cellar was definitely off limits. The stories I had heard about the house as a child were not far from my thoughts, and I never felt comfortable while living there. After a couple of months, Nan wanted to come back to her house, and my cousin put a bed downstairs for her and Aunty Gladys to sleep. We were able to stay upstairs, but it didn't work out as Nan didn't like any noise and was often cross with me, which was so unlike the Nan I knew. I tried to keep the children quiet, which was also tough on them because they were not particularly noisy children anyway. I feel quite sad reflecting on this time and wonder if I could have done something more to help Nan, but I was a young mum looking after my family, and they were my priority at that time. Nan ended up living with my cousin and his wife, and they looked after her till she died, which they did with a lot of love and devotion, and I shall always be grateful to them. My love and respect for Nan didn't falter during this time, and I was very sorry and sad when she passed away in 1978. RIP Nan xx

Nan on Fleetwood beach

CHAPTER SIX

Aunties and Uncles

"When trouble comes, it's your family that supports you"
Guy Lafleur

IN THE EARLY DAYS, ALL of my aunties and uncles played a part in our lives. On my Dad's side, we had two aunties and one uncle. Aunty Margaret was the eldest of the family, followed by Uncle Ken and then Aunty Beat (Beatrice). They, too, were a close family with Aunty Margaret being the matriarch, and like us, they had endured many family tragedies. They lost their mum when she was only forty years old, and their brother William Henry was lost at sea when he was twenty-three. Aunty Marg looked after them all when their mother died, and Dad was only seven and the youngest. I think they must have been quite protective of him and they remained close to him after he married and had his own family. Aunty Marg lived in Oxford Road for all of her married life, and we often visited her, it was me that usually stayed at her house when we needed looking after and I use to enjoy these times. Her husband Matthew had also died young, and I never knew him. Matthew was Aunty Marg's second husband, so both husbands had died early in their marriages, not unlike her ancestors had.

Aunty Beat lived in Seabank Road, which was not too far from us, her house was near to the beach, so we visited her often and was always made welcome. I remember her lovely smiling eyes and the kindness she showed us. Her husband William (Uncle Bill) was a fisherman, and I remember him well. They always made us welcome, and we enjoyed going to their house. They kept a parrot for many years who talked a lot and was noisy, but we were all fascinated with him and would try to get him to speak to us. When the coalman came, he used to say "three bags please," and the parrot sounded just like him. It didn't matter that they might have only wanted one bag The coalman got used to the parrots voice in the end and always checked to see how many bags they wanted. We were close to our cousins and spent many happy hours on the Mount and the beach playing with the younger family members. I was in the hospital having my appendix out when my cousin Margaret got married, and she came to see me in her wedding gown. The whole ward enjoyed her visit, and of course, she looked beautiful as all brides do. I'm proud that we remain close to our cousins, even today, which I feel is a measure of the closeness our family had always maintained.

We never had much to do with Uncle Ken, my dad's brother, and I'm not sure why. He was always okay with us as children, but we never got gifts or cards from him, unlike my Aunties, who always bought us birthday presents. It didn't matter that we didn't receive presents, it was nothing about that, but it shows there was never a relationship between our families. I can only ever remember visiting him once or twice despite the fact he lived only two streets away from us, and I'm not sure of the relationship he had with my Dad. When we did visit him, I remember thinking he looked like my Dad, but Dad was much more handsome. It was such a shame he wasn't involved in our lives as it may have helped us all to have this male link to my Dad.

My Mum had three sisters, and Aunty Vera was the eldest. When I was very young, Aunty Vera lived at Nan's and had since she was first married. They moved to the new West View estate in about 1955 and had a lovely council house in Calder Avenue. I missed her when she went, and although it was still in Fleetwood, it may have been on another planet to me, as it seemed so far away. I use to visit her often though; in fact, I use to love staying with her when Uncle Jim was at sea. Her house was always clean and tidy, she cooked excellent meals, and we had a mug of cocoa together at night before going to bed. My cousin John was my Aunty Vera's only son, and I can remember hanging out with him when they lived at Nan's. We collected empty pop bottles to take back to the shop as you got money refunded for returning them in those days. I'm not sure what sort of assistant I was to him, but I liked getting a sixpence now and then. I loved John, he was older than us and played the guitar, he was in a band called The Unknowns, but far from being unknown they were very popular and had quite a following. John was the nearest thing I would ever get to see a star in person, and I use to love hearing him play. He was mad keen on Buddy Holly, and I remember him being terribly upset when he heard the news Buddy Holly had died. I always think of John when I hear a Buddy Holly song, and this takes me right back to Calder Avenue and my lovely Aunty Vera. Nan had a small black dog called Paddy who we all adored, especially John, and we all made a fuss over him. I think it must have been Nan's Irish heritage which made her call him Paddy, and I can still remember his adorable face and that wagging tail. We all loved having John in our lives, he was like an older brother, and he never seemed to get annoyed with any of us.

I was playing out one day when I was staying with Aunty Vera, and I had been trying to balance like a gymnast on the small wall outside of her house. I fell off the wall grazing the inside of my wrist which produced the tiniest amount of blood. I had been told by one of my friends if blood came from those veins in your wrist, you would surely bleed to death. I screamed like a banshee as I laid there dying till Aunty Vera came running out to see what was the matter and calm me down. It took a long time before I believed Aunty Vera that I wasn't going to bleed to death, but she eventually managed to stop me crying with the aid of a biscuit or two. Uncle Jim, her husband, was a nice man, and he was also a fisherman who always had a twinkle in his eye. He made jokes about everything and anything, and I think John has his sense of humour even to this day.

Aunty Vera often loaned money to my mum as she felt sorry for us, and I hated taking the dreaded note to her asking to lend a pound, so we could get something for our tea. Tea more often than not consisted of chips and bread and butter; the pound also got mum a packet of cigarettes. My Auntie Vera also smoked as did my Auntie Gladys and Nan; Aunty Myra was the only one of the girls that didn't. Poor Aunty Vera got cancer and died in 1963 and she was such a loss to us; I shall never forget her. I remember when she was terminally ill, and her bed was downstairs, she wanted to go to the toilet, and mum was in the kitchen. Because Aunty Vera was unable to get out of bed she had to use a bedpan.I will never forget her looking at me as I helped her and she said, "thanks love, you would make a good nurse." I did not know then I would be putting many people onto bedpans in the future. That is the last memory I have of Aunty Vera, who I will always remember with love.

Aunty Gladys was the second eldest and she never married. She was a massive smoker and this eventually took its toll on her life. Aunty Glad had a kind heart and was funny; in fact, I can still hear the sound of her laughing, which always ended up in a coughing fit. I think Aunty Gladys was a gadget person, and I have probably got my love of technical gadgets from her. I can remember her buying a machine that scraped new potatoes, which was a job I, in particular, hated. You placed the potatoes in a drum with water and turned the handle to agitate the potatoes. The potatoes got scraped on the drums rough lining which took the skins off; I thought it was magic. She also bought a knitting machine which we all benefitted from by making jumpers and cardigans for us. Aunty Gladys had a couple of jobs, one was a braider making and mending fishing nets and the other as a barmaid at the Prince Arthur, on the corner of Lord Street and Warren Street. Nan also cleaned there on occasions, and I loved going to work with her in the mornings. I had to wipe the tables and arrange the bottles on the shelves, and she always opened a bottle of pop to drink as a reward. In the early days the barrels of beer would be delivered by horse and cart and rolled into the cellar. It was exciting to watch, and many children gathered, keen to see the horse as well as to watch the spectacle of barrels being rolled down into the cellar. There was also a snug, with the entrance being on Warren Street. It was a tiny room with a bar at the end and it had long leather seats either side of the small space; it smelt of leather, beer, and cigarettes. The snug was for ladies only, and I remember my Nan going in there some nights. There were stringent laws about kids going into pubs, so we just use to peek through the door and watch them drinking their beer, which I think might have been Stout. Aunty Glad also worked at another pub in Warren Street called the Ship and the only thing I can remember about it was the many rooms above the bar area. It is now flats for the nautical college students, which I am pleased about and quite fitting for a fishing town.

At least that was one building that hasn't been demolished. Aunty Glad died of throat cancer in 1984, and she too was lovingly cared for by my cousin John and his wife May in the weeks before her death. There can be no doubt that John has been a great advocate for Nan and our aunties and has always cared for them as a son would, and I'm sure Aunty Vera would have been proud of him.

Aunty Myra was the youngest daughter and was quite glamorous when she was younger. I remember her dressing up for her nights out when she went dancing in the Blackpool Tower ballroom. Her clothes were lovely and modern for those times, her flared skirts and net underskirts must have looked fabulous when she danced. Aunty Myra and Uncle Bob married in 1955, and they also lived with Nan. They used the parlour as their living room and had the small bedroom at the back of the house. Uncle Bob was a fisherman, and I think he always did well, sailing in ships that usually made good money. I liked Uncle Bob, he was kind to us, and we looked forward to the times he was in from sea.

His smile was always gummy because for some reason he would not put his dentures in; I'm not sure why. We were used to seeing him like that, and it didn't matter to anyone at all. They had two boys, and I loved their firstborn; I use to take him all over in his pram, which looking back must have been an excellent help to Aunty Myra. I would walk around the prom and onto the Mount, keeping him out for hours. He was such a good baby and no trouble to look after. Uncle Bob's mother and father use to visit my Nan's quite often, and I got to know them well. His mother was a serious-looking lady, and I much preferred his father, although there may have been an ulterior motive for my fondness of him. One day when they were leaving my Nan's, I innocently walked them to the end of the street, and as we passed the corner shop, his father gave me some money to buy sweets. Of course, now I always wanted to walk to the corner every time they visited until someone, not sure who, worked my plan out and put a stop to it. Whenever I talked to Aunty Myra about our lives, I got the feeling she never understand the hardship Mum went through, and always thought Mum could have done better with her money.

I have said it before though, she didn't have to walk in her shoes and her life was quite different to Mum's. I think there was a little bit of angst as they got older, and Mum use to say, "I'm not going to bingo tonight as

Myra is going, so I won't stand a chance." I think what that meant, rightly or wrongly, she saw Aunty Myra as being luckier than her. Aunty Myra died in 2018 in her late 80's, the last survivor from mum's family, and I can hear my Mum saying "well, she would be, wouldn't she." I certainly loved my Aunties, as each was unique in their own way. I can sum up their attributes; kindness, loyalty, and love of family. How lucky we were to have had them so near to us, and to be such a big part of our early lives.

CHAPTER SEVEN

My School Years

"Education is not preparation for life; education is life itself"

John Dewy

I LOVED SCHOOL RIGHT FROM day one at five years old through to my last day when I was fifteen. Initially, I loved the routine of school, eating school dinners, and playing with my friends. In later years the challenge of trying to get out of a *C* class to a *B* class was fundamental to me as I wanted to do well. I had experienced quite a bit of time off school due to a grumbling appendix, which had affected my progress through my early years. I eventually had my appendix removed when I was eight, but I had spent a lot of time away from school. I had a lot of time to make up for my absences' and I remember trying to get to grips with long division math. The teacher had to spend extra time with me at her desk to help me catch up on the work I had missed but it was an awful experience. Every time I got the long division sum wrong, she would slap the back of my legs. Her bullying had such a negative impact on me that I never mastered long division until my adult years. I didn't want to go to school one particular morning so I told Mum about the teacher, and how she kept slapping my legs. Mum was very angry with her, and had thought it was unusual that I didn't want to go to school. Mum put on her coat and immediately went to school with me in tow. I dreaded facing the teacher as I had told on her and I thought she would slap me even more. Mum spoke to the teacher, or should I say shouted at the teacher, and she never hit again. A tutor at the school where I worked in Auckland many years later coached me in math for my Nursing Degree in 1993, and even though I didn't particularly need to know long division, I had told him the story so he showed me how to do it, and I realised it was quite easy.

Jennifer age five

My primary school was Blakiston Street School, and I remember my first day like it was yesterday. Mum took me into the classroom, and the teacher said to take a box of alphabet bricks to the desk, pointing to its direction. I took the box over to the desk and then took it straight back to her. The teacher said, "they are for you to play with," but I thought I just had to take it to the table and back, I must have been a very concrete thinker at five years old! The teachers were lovely, and I had a happy time in that school. Christmas was a particularly exciting time of the year, we sang carols, watched rehearsals for the Nativity and helped to make Christmas decorations to put up around the school. I always wanted to be in the Nativity play, and I loved the story which I knew inside out. I could just see myself as Mary but was never chosen and I wonder if I had set my ambitions too high. Maybe if I had volunteered to be a shepherd or a wise man, I would have got a part. My sisters Margaret and Patricia were both angels in the Nativity at one stage, and I have to say they both looked quite angelic and did an excellent job, but it never happened for me.

I must have been accident-prone as a child because another catastrophe happened while I was at Blakiston school. I fell up the steps leading into school, hitting my forehead. I sustained a gash that needed stitches, and I still have the scar. As usual, I screamed and screamed, especially when I put my fingers onto my forehead and it felt like I had a big hole in it. There is a photo of Blakiston Street school, which often appears on a social media page I belong to, and you can see the steps I fell up. I always smile at the thought of my wailing and the teachers trying to sort me out.

My middle school was Chaucer Road School, and fortunately for me, many of my friends from Blakiston also went to that school. We use to play all sorts of games at playtime, and one particular game stays in my mind. A group of us would pretend to fly on a trapeze, putting our arms in the air and running past each other as free as birds. Sounds silly I know but we loved playing it. We also played tag and skipped with plastic ropes which hurt your legs if you got caught in them. I had lots of friends at school, and at this age, it didn't matter what you had or whether you were rich or poor. But as I got older, I didn't have a lot of friends, I knew a lot of girls, but I didn't consider them my special friends. I can't say I was a popular girl at school, and I always felt it was because we were from a struggling family, especially after losing Dad. We had delicious school dinners, and I loved them, they cost five shillings each week, and when Dad died, they became free. Not having to pay for our school dinners would have been a relief for my Mum, but for me, it was just another sign that we were poor. Around 1130am, the smell of the school dinners would come wafting into the classrooms, making my mouth water and tummy growl with anticipation, and the bell couldn't come quick enough. We ate our dinners in the school hall, and as soon as the bell sounded, there was a frenzied dash to wash our hands. We had to get in line and have our hands examined with the critical eyes of the dinner ladies, and if you hadn't cleaned them well enough, you had to go back to the washroom. The dinner ladies took over from the teachers to keep us in order, and they were very kind. They walked around the tables to make sure we were eating everything and would tell you off if your mouth was open as you ate or you had your elbows on the table. I was very compliant on all of those counts because if there was food over, then I wanted to be chosen for seconds. The school also sold biscuits at break time, jammy dodgers, and chocolate fingers. I was unable to buy every day because Mum wouldn't give money to one if she couldn't give it to us all so we seldom purchased them. The Co-Op on the way to school use to sell their broken biscuits, and you could get quite a big bag for the same amount of money spent at school, but they were plain biscuits, not often chocolate, and they were not available every day. We also got a bottle of milk every day at school, lovely in the winter when it was icy cold but awful when it was warm in the summer. The warm milk put me off milk for the rest of my life, and although I now have milk on cereal, I would never be able to drink a glass of milk or have it in my tea. One thing I didn't like about school was when the school nurse (nitty Norah) came to visit. We would all line up, and she would start to look in your hair as if she was a detective looking for a murder weapon. Everyone stood waiting to see what colour letter you got, and although I can't remember the colours, mine was always the coloured one given out for having nits, so everyone would know you had them. There was a great shame in having nits in those days, and to me, it felt like another indicator highlighting my social standing.

My last two years spent at Bailey Secondary Modern were happy ones. My favourite subject was English and History, and there was one teacher in particular that I liked called Miss Dawson, who taught English. I was a model student in her class, and I nearly always came top of the class in this subject. I don't think with respect my Mum really rated how vital our education was and she would often keep us at home to look after the young ones. I resented this as a teenager, so it was often left to Jan to stay home as she was not as verbal as I was. Mum didn't like any arguments, so I think it would have been easier to bypass me. Fortunately, it didn't stop Jan pursuing her career as a nurse, where it might have been a different story for me. I did make it to a B class in the end, and I was in the top class at Whiteacre, a boarding school I attended, so I am proud of those achievements. I am, of course, less impressive of my antics in reaching them.

Bailey school was a large building with a formidable facade. It was the grounding establishment for many Fleetwood children who either loved it or hated it. I am proud to say I loved it there and was very sad to leave when I was fifteen. The school had a boy's side and a girl's side, and they only mixed at the end of the year for the school dance which was held in the hall. A couple of weeks before the end of term, we had to practice waltzing and other dances in preparation for the event. Although I loved to dance, the boys seldom chose me. I always ended up sitting with the other girls who had been overlooked. I felt obliged to look on with hope that one of the boys would walk over and ask me to dance but it never happened. In the end, the deserted girls had to dance together and for some reason, I always took the lead. To this day I always take the lead when Dave and I dance together. It is no wonder poor Dave finds it hard to dance with me, but old habits die hard. Unfortunately, they demolished the school and built new houses on the site. Another part of history has gone; it would have made a magnificent community building as it held lots of happy and sometimes not so happy memories for many Fleetwood people. I dreaded leaving school as it was my salvation, I worked hard in my classes and I abided by the rules. One could say it was all in vain because sadly I was not able to stay at school to do my O levels. It took me a further twenty-two years to achieve the five O levels I needed to pursue my career as a Registered Nurse, but I did do it in the end.

CHAPTER EIGHT

Happy Days

"One of the luckiest things that can happen to you in life is, I think, to have a happy childhood"

Agatha Christie

MY LIFE THROUGHOUT THE EARLY fifties was one of relative calm spending our days on the beach and waiting for dad to come in from sea. Nan and our aunties who lived next door played a big part in our lives and looking back, and as an adult, I thank God they were there for us. I think they provided a safe, stable environment for us while our lives swung between one of being broke to joyous periods when Dad was home, and there was money in the pot, Mum was happy, and we seemed to have everything. We did have many happy times as children, and I loved Warren Street, we were near the beach, shops, and the cinemas, and as a child, you couldn't wish for anything better. I'm not sure if the weather has changed over the years, or I have rose-coloured glasses on, but our summers were hot and long with thunderstorms that would light up the sky. Dad was in from sea when we had a particular storm that stayed in my memory. We were on the beach; Mum and Dad had gone out as it was his landing day. When the storm arrived, it poured with rain, and the thunder hurt our ears, we were all very frightened. We ran to shelter in the verandas under the baths huddling together to ensure the lightning didn't strike us. We kept looking over to the road trying to put on a brave face, waiting for someone to rescue us. We must have looked like abandoned orphans all huddled together, and if the lightning had of hit us, we would have all died together. There were not many cars on the road in those days, but sure enough, a taxi pulled up with our knights in shining armour, aka Mum and Dad, who knew we would all be scared. We did get a ride home in the taxi, which was a treat for us, and the ride home almost made up for being frightened in the storm.

Dad's time in from sea went quickly, and the pattern was always the same. There would be the excitement of getting a telemac to say he was coming in from sea at a specific time on a particular day, landing day, then the goodbye day. The telemac had the time of high water stamped on it, so we knew what time to watch the boat come down the channel. Because Fleetwood is tidal, knowing the height of the tide gave the skipper a window of opportunity to come down the channel safely. If they missed the tide, they would have to wait at Wyre Light till the next tide, twelve hours later. It took the trawlers about thirty minutes to come from Wyre Light into Fleetwood dock, and it was a wonderful sight to see trawler after trawler sailing down the channel to be greeted by loved ones, thrilled to see them return. How excited the men themselves must have been, some would have been longing for a beer and others to see their wives and girlfriends. Dave told me they would all be happy and whistling as they showered (many for the first time since leaving the port) and packed their bags. We have stood on the Ferry beach many times, waiting to catch a glimpse of Dad, who was often in the wheelhouse. We would be so excited to see him waving to us, and he would sound the trawlers siren as he passed us. A statue on the promenade at Fleetwood depicts a lady and child waving to her loved one on the boats, which is lovely, and brings back so many memories of the years I did this. There are often flowers in her hands or by her side, and it's nice to know our brave Fleetwood trawlermen are remembered to this day.

I think it is fitting to write about Wyre Light as I don't think it will be visible for much longer. Wyre Light is the burnt-out lighthouse at the beginning of the channel marking the navigation channel to the town. A blind Irish engineer designed the lighthouse, which was one of the first screw-pile lighthouses ever to be built. It was an essential structure for the safety of shipping entering the channel and a welcome sight for

Fleetwood fishermen returning from their trips away. The Wyre Light, along with a pair of onshore lighthouses, Beach lighthouse, and Pharos lighthouse, provided a navigational guide to shipping entering the Wyre estuary. Their beams aligned with each other, but sadly Wyre light has not been party to this for many years. There was a time you could walk out to Wyre Light, but unfortunately, with the changing sands and tidal currents, it is now too dangerous. The lighthouse has succumbed to the weather and turbulence of the tides, and sadly it collapsed in 2017. The wreck of this much-loved lighthouse has continued to deteriorate, but no one will admit ownership, and its upkeep was abandoned many years ago. Today it is scarcely visible, and when it eventually surrenders to its burial ground, it will be a sad loss and another icon from Fleetwood's rich maritime history to have faded into the past.

The day after a trawler came in from sea, the fish was landed and sold on the fish market to be transported all over the UK. Sometimes Dad made excellent trips where he picked up a decent amount of money, and at other times, he picked up very little. It was a hard life for the fishermen as they were treated as casuals and had no guarantee of work. They had to earn money for the Company, or they were out of a ship; there were no guarantees of a job from one fishing trip to another. The day Dad landed; he went down to the dock at about 7 am. They gave each fisherman a couple of fish that they could keep or sell, but Dad usually sold his, especially if he knew they had a poor catch. We use to take turns to go with Dad down to get his fish and money, which we all wanted to do, as the other fishermen would give you money as a treat. Dad always went in a taxi, and his regular taxi driver was Harold Wright, who was a lovely man. Being a taxi driver in Fleetwood during those years was an industry in itself. Most of the fishermen had their specific driver who would be hired for the duration of their time ashore. The taxi driver would accompany them to the pubs and go wherever they wanted to go. After Dad got his money, he would come home and get ready to go out with Mum, usually to the pubs, of which there were many in Fleetwood. They came back in the late afternoon for tea and then often went out again for the evening if they had the money. If Dad had made a good trip, then this day would be spent with us at Blackpool, or he would take us out for tea. The following day he would leave again, and if this were in the daytime, we would go to the Ferry beach to wave him goodbye. Dad loved his family, and I can remember sitting on his knee, he use to let us brush his hair and we all squabbled to find a place on his knee. I was always proud of the fact my Dad thought I had lovely handwriting as he asked me to copy all his fishing notes into a new hard-backed book. I was excited and proud to do this job for him, and it took many weeks in between his trips for me to complete it. I also remember getting the slipper off him (smacked with it) for throwing bits of soil at a door where the aged pensioners lived, then hiding from them. Wow did I get a hiding from him, he was so angry that I could disrespect the elderly like that.

We moved to Wingrove Road in about 1957, and although it seemed so far from my Nans, we quite liked it there. It was a young family area, and we met and played with lots of children, all with various standards of living. One of our favourite games was waving to the trams that passed the bottom of our street, as we had seen the actors do in the Railway Children, a television programme. We all sat on the wall dressed up in long dresses and hats waving to the passengers who nearly always waved back. My best friend was the second eldest of five children and lived a few doors away. We use to do most things together and would often sleepover at each other's house. She attended a dancing school which I thought was quite swanky and we both dressed up in her costumes. Janet arranged concerts in our back garden putting blankets over the line as curtains that could part and reveal the singer or dancer. The boys helped with the curtains as they didn't want to participate in the concert. Many of the kids in the neighbourhood came and watched our shows. They sat on makeshift seats their eager faces looking forward to the entertainment. Looking back, they were such happy times. One of our favourite places to play was on the cornfield, a big piece of land at the top of our street, and it attracted many kids from the neighbourhood. News that the grass had been cut spread like wildfire, and all the kids converged onto the field. We threw the grass in the air, rolled in it, and generally had fun throwing it at each other. We also played outside in the evenings, playing rounders, hide and seek, knock a door run, skipping and skating. I loved the long summer evenings as we would sometimes play out till 10 pm, and I always hated having to go home to bed. I am still in contact with my friend and her brothers from Wingrove Road, and when we are together, we laugh at our memories and remind each other about the times we may have forgotten and the good times we had.

My own children many years later proved good at entertaining the neighbourhood and when we lived in NZ, the house we built initially had no fences up. I was sat having a coffee and to my surprise I saw a small pony passing the window. My girls had enlisted a girl who owned a pony to take childrenon a ride around the house. It was obviously popular as most of the kids from the neighbourhood were waiting in a queue. Sam who at this stage was a budding gymnast (not that we realized this at this time) was entertaining the crowd performing back flips.

Just Harry missing, taken outside our house in Warren Street

Despite the financial hardship we lived in, we were happy children and had many opportunities to go on trips with other children. Dad must have been a member of various clubs around Fleetwood, and members children could go on coach trips to places like Chester Zoo, the illuminations at Blackpool, and the Tower Circus. I loved these trips on the coaches where we would get sweets and pop supplied to us. On one of the trips to Chester Zoo, we had spending money for ice-cream and sweets, but when we arrived at the zoo, the first thing we saw at the entrance was a beautiful, rather large, St Bernard dog. The dog attracted us straight away, and we noticed it had a charity barrel around its neck. The little band of Gorst kids stopped to stroke the dog and, at that point, made the catastrophic decision to put all of our spending money into the barrel because the dog looked so sad (as only St Bernard dogs can). This act of kindness resulted in an afternoon of watching all the other children enjoying their ice-creams and sweets with envy. Thankfully we loved looking at all the zoo animals, which saved the day, and we still enjoyed ourselves. In any event, how can you compare sweets and ice-cream with a lost climber on Mount Everest who would have benefited from our donation by saving his life! I'm not sure if it was on this outing but when we were pulling into Fleetwood train station, the train didn't slow down enough and we hit the barrier. This caused us all to be thrown forward which resulted in some of the children sustaining minor injuries. I was told the driver had his leg chopped off and so I fainted, something I did a lot as a child. The news spread around Fleetwood quickly and many mothers and fathers converged on the station, including Mum and Dad who were relieved to see us all intact.

As we were growing up over the years there were three separate periods to our lives, which repeated over and over again. Waiting with joy and excitement for dad to come in from sea, enjoying our time with him when he was home, and then saying goodbye to him with a sinking sadness in our hearts. Those periods continued for me until 1969 with my husband Dave, a fisherman, that was until we hatched a plan that changed our lives forever, an idea, which I now see, could have been planted in my head by my mother when I was a very young girl. These are my happy memories where I thought my world was perfect, living in a unique bubble, cared for, and loved, where nothing nasty rarely happened. Still, unfortunately, these bubbles can burst, it's no one's fault, you never expect it, call it fate or whatever, but when my bubble burst, it was devastating to me and everyone in my family. My lovely Dad was lost at sea along with all his shipmates, and we would never see him again.

CHAPTER NINE

A Tragedy Unfolds

"And once the storm is over, you won't remember how you made it through, how you managed to survive. You won't even be sure whether the storm is really over. But one thing is certain. When you come out of the storm, you won't be the same person who walked in. That's what this storm's all about"

Haruki Murakami

ALTHOUGH I HAVE HAPPY MEMORIES of Wingrove Road, where we had lots of fun with friends that I will always treasure, our lives were changing, and one terrible event brought our lives to a crashing standstill just before Christmas, 1959 when Dad's ship was lost at sea. Emotionally it was devastating to us all. He had left six children ranging from two to thirteen, and my Mum a widow at only thirty-five.

Dad should have come in from sea in the early hours of the morning, and I remember that day as if it was yesterday. I got up for school that morning expecting Dad to be home, but Mum said they had missed the tide and not to worry as he would be home when we got in from school. I thought she was joking as she often said this, and then Dad would jump out from behind a door to surprise us, but not this time. I couldn't wait to get home from school that afternoon to see my Dad, and I remember while walking home from school, down Lingfield Road, having a sickly feeling in my stomach. I thought this feeling was excitement, but a thought in my head kept saying "I wouldn't know what to do if anything ever happened to my Dad." Five minutes later, I was in the house looking at my distraught mother and aunties along with the Mission man Duncan Brown. At that moment I knew something was seriously wrong, and I was dreading Mum's next words. Mum said Dad's boat was missing, but there was still hope, that a search was underway, and would continue until they found the ship. I knew though, don't ask me how, it may have been the serious upset faces that surrounded me or that nagging sickening feeling I'd had on my way home, but whatever it was, I knew I would never see my Dad again.

Funny, but I can't remember crying, I felt the pain, and my heart ached, but I don't think I cried. As young as Janet and I were, we had to protect the younger ones, and we had to be brave for them. They didn't understand what was happening around them, and I'm sure inside they would have been scared seeing everyone's sad face. We had many visitors, friends, and family, but a blackness hung over the house while we waited for news of a rescue with anticipation. There had been a search in the South Minch, and we didn't have to wait long for news because there was no sign of the ship. It was presumed to have been overwhelmed in heavy seas as she made her way home, a journey she had made many times before. The Red Falcon was lost with all hands leaving twenty-five children without a father and no hope of us ever seeing Dad again. They found some wreckage washed up twenty-five miles north of the ship's last known position, which including a rocket container box, floorboards off a lifeboat, and two lifebuoys stamped *Red Falcon*. Seven months after the loss, an inquiry opened at Fleetwood Town Hall, and it found the last radio contact with the *Red Falcon* was at 7 am on December 14th. The investigation believed it was difficult to ascertain the cause of the loss, but the most probable cause was that the ship was overwhelmed, but its loss left Fleetwood devastated with shock and grief.

It was a strange environment to be in and as young as we were there was no laughter in our house, even the younger ones were subdued. The whole of Fleetwood waited with us, drawn together as it had many times before when a trawler was overdue. It was a week before Christmas and the town seemed silent, too stunned to celebrate the usual festivities. My Aunty Myra was in Milton Lodge having her first baby when the news of

Dad came. They tried to keep the news from her for at least twenty-four hours, but it was inevitable she would find out. Within days an appeal fund for dependents was set up by the Mayor of Fleetwood. The owners, Iago, started the fund off with a £1,000 donation, and it eventually topped £20,000, with cash pouring in from all over the country.

When all hope had gone, we would talk about the possibility of Dad being on a desert island and that a ship would pass by and rescue him. Such are the thoughts of an eleven-year-old and such was the way we wanted to give hope to our younger brothers and sisters. People were kind, and we managed to get through Christmas, but our lives would never be the same, and this eleven-year-old had to grow up very quickly. The loss of my Dad's ship, the Red Falcon, was pivotal to how our lives changed, and it set us on a new course that had many storm clouds.

The public was indeed very sympathetic regarding the loss of the *Red Falcon*, and I know mum received many cards containing money, which would have helped her in the weeks that followed. Uncle Bill, Auntie Beat's husband, bought us all new shoes as Dads' money that trip, had been earmarked to have our old shoes replaced. Our family was one of the larger families, and everyone tried to help at that time. The Mission man Duncan Brown stood by us steadfastly for many years, helping wherever he could and taking an interest in all we did. We had to carry on, though, and that is what we did through those bad times. We were a close family, and I'm proud of this and all which we achieved despite the adversity we faced.

Red Falcon

CHAPTER TEN

A Life Without Dad

*"Losing my father at such an early age is the scar of my soul.
But I feel like it ultimately made me into the person I am today.
I understand the journey of life, and I had to go through what
I did to be here"*

Anonymous

SO, THERE WE HAVE IT, my lovely Dad had gone forever, my bubble
had burst, and life would never be the same for us. People were kind, and
the school did all they could to see we were dealing with our loss, but it
was hard, and the future seemed so uncertain without Dad. It must have
been terrible for Mum, wondering how she would cope with six children,
how she would manage her finances when we were already struggling.
Mum would have been missing her husband, her man, and the love of
her life.

About a year after Dad was lost, we moved to Heathfield Road to
a five bedroomed council house, we were all growing up, and three
bedrooms was just not enough space for us all. Heathfield Road did have
a bit of a reputation for being a rough area, and at first, I use to hate saying
where I lived. The house was spacious though, and we were able to spread
out. Janet, Tricia and me had a bedroom each which was a luxury for us.
Most of the neighbours, like us, had huge families and were continually
living on the breadline but I can honestly say they were the salt of the

earth and would do anything to help each other. We soon became part of the Heathfield Road clan. Our house was very social as we were growing up, we were allowed to bring friends home, and Mum had a few lodgers, which helped her financially, so there was always something going on. Mum worked at the Marine Hall as the catering manageress, her hours were long and she often came home looking weary. Jan and I had to look after the younger children and keep the house tidy, which was no mean feat. The laundry pile alone was like a mountain, and we didn't have a washing machine. Mum use to hired a twin-tub washing machine when she either had enough money or when we were running out of clothes. A young lad delivered the washing machine, and Janet had a crush on him. We always made fun of her crush, and we would tease her when we knew he was coming. I don't think the lad had any idea of this, and we have laughed about it since. I should imagine, the washer boy would have run a mile if confronted with the knowledge of a possible romance with one of the Gorst girls. I have since wondered if the washing machine ever worked again after spending the day with us and being filled at least twenty times. It must have been worked to death getting through the piles of washing and we certainly got our monies worth; the only downside was all the ironing the next day.

We lived from payday to payday with some borrowing of money in between, and none of us liked to be the one who had to take a note to the designated chosen one. When I look back, Mum did try her best to give us a good Christmas, decent clothes, and food on the table, but we often went without, and we got used to it. Because we were fatherless, the term they used in those days, a couple of opportunities came my way. I got school dinners for free and a chance to go to a boarding school called Whiteacre, located near Clitheroe. Being chosen to go to Whiteacre was left to the discretion of the headmistress, and I was desperate to go there. I had to get permission from Miss Black, the headmistress, which I dreaded. Even the thought of facing Miss Black made me shake, and nearly everyone avoided any interaction with her. She was a frightening figure who could make your life at school a misery, and we were all scared of her. Janet had done a few weeks at Whiteacre the year before but had to return home in the middle of the term to look after us all, so when I asked the headmistress if I could go to Whiteacre, she exploded. Her face was like thunder as she shouted *"no you cannot go."* She stated the reason being was that Janet hadn't completed the full term, and it was doubtful that I would. I felt disappointed and devastated, but you did not argue with her, and I had no other option but to accept her decision, even though I thought it was totally unjustified.

I was doing well at school and loved it, my attendance at school was excellent. If Mum wanted to keep me at home for any reason I use to cry and say it was unfair. I put up such a performance that she gave up keeping me at home so she must have thought the fuss I made was not worth it. I was not too fond of the responsibility of the house and cleaning in fact I loathed it. I guess as a teenager, I was fighting against all the responsibility that seemed to be put on us from an early age. I wanted to be like my friends who had a Mum and Dad, food cooked for them and clean clothes every day, how I envied their lives. I wish this wasn't true, but it was, and although with hindsight I wish I had been a better daughter, I wasn't, so I have to live with that. As I got older, I did try to make up for my turbulent teenage years and helped Mum as much as I could. I did, however, love my family and always looked out for the younger ones. I never left them on their own, and took them with me when I went out, so I suppose I wasn't all bad. One day at school, shortly after the blasting I got from the headmistress regarding the boarding school fiasco, I got a message that Miss Black wanted to see me straight away in her office. My heart sunk, and I was terrified, I was trying to think had I done something wrong. I waited outside her office, hands behind my back and shaking in my shoes. When she called me into her office, she stared at me with her piercing eyes and said she had thought about my request and told me I could go to Whiteacre after all, but if I dared to leave before the full term, then there would be serious consequences. I was over the moon and very excited at the thought of going, and if it had not been for her forbearing manner, I think I would have hugged her. Now I am older and reflecting on this event, I wonder if the teachers may have said something to her about the decision not to let me go to Whiteacre because there wasn't an acceptable reason. There is no doubt that Jan's attendance record was poor, and she was kept away from school at the drop of a hat. To be fair I couldn't have helped her situation with my reluctance to stay home and maybe share those days with her. I do think Miss Black knew Jan was required to look after everyone, and that she didn't have a choice. Many years later, she asked Janet to her house on Beach Road and gave her some letters from Mum regarding Dad's loss. Miss Black had kept the letters for many years, and I think this provided a connection between them both. A few years later, Miss Black died in the hospital where Janet worked and she held her hand while she was so ill. I think Miss Black would have been very pleased that Janet was with her.

As I got older and was able to be more responsible for myself, life started to change, and although I'm not sure if I was always happy, I just had to get on with it. Our lives were considerably different since we lost Dad. I loved my siblings, but as a teenager, I wanted more fun like all my friends seemed to be having. Although I did come around to doing more jobs at home, I know I did them with menace. Sometimes Auntie Myra came to sort us out while Mum was at work, which I dreaded. She would dish out jobs for us all to do and as per usual I never wanted to do them. I remember running down the backstreet at Heathfield Road with Auntie Myra pursuing me because I had refused to do what she wanted me to do. I must have been so frustrating to them. I did talk to Aunty Myra about this incident last time I was home, and we both laughed together although she didn't laugh at the time. There was another time when Mum wanted me to dry the dishes, and as usual, I did not want to do it. I came up with all sorts of excuses, one being that I couldn't find the tea towel, which would have been correct because usually they were all dirty. A very annoyed Mum shouted for me to "hang them on the line then," so I did. It took me ages to put them on the line, and I secured them with pegs, hoping that I didn't break anything. Mum came to see what I was doing and when she saw the cups and plates hanging there, she couldn't stop laughing, which was lucky for me. There is no doubt our lives had changed with the extra responsibilities that were handed to us when Dad died but we did our best, it's a pity my best was sometimes just not good enough. Those years of hardship intermingled with love, laughter, and tears are worth remembering, and in spite of those hardships, we grew up into respectful kind adults.

CHAPTER ELEVEN

A Young Widow

"She stood in the storm, and when the wind did not blow her way, she adjusted her sails."

Elizabeth Edwards

WHEN I GOT OLDER, I realized the ramifications of what Dad's loss had on Mum. She was only thirty-five, with six children ranging from two to thirteen. Mum had no income apart from a widow's pension and that much-needed family allowance. There had been a fund set up for the widows and children of the Red Falcon disaster, but it was held in trust for our future and was not able to be accessed until we were twenty-one. (I think this was the age). It wasn't a lot of money by today's standards, but it was needed, and it did help at that time.

Mum was successful in appealing the fund based on the fact that money was needed while we were growing up, not when we were older and able to fend for ourselves. I think that must have been how she survived those years, and I didn't blame her for using it. I know by the time I got married I had approximately £100 left from the fund which just about paid for my wedding. Mum worked hard and did long hours at the Marine Hall, and she was good at her job. It gave her an identity other than being a mum with six children to look after. For us, the work of caring for our younger siblings took on a new significance, we had no other choice, and I tried to fill that role. Unfortunately, there were periods of unwillingness on my part as I wanted a bit of fun in my life, but I had to help out and get on with it. There were specific jobs we had to get done before Mum got home from work, and so between playing and arguing who was to do which task, we somehow managed to get them done. We often just completed them by the skin of our teeth just before Mum got home. Someone would-be put-on guard to watch for the bus, which would have dropped Mum off around the corner on Hatfield Avenue. Then a two-minute warning would be issued so we could sweep the floor and put the tools of our trade away before Mum walked from the bus stop. Mum often worked late, and I'm sure she would have been exhausted most of the time, something I wouldn't have given a thought to.

I know in my heart Mum tried her hardest to give us a happy childhood after Dad died and provide us with clothes and items deemed necessary to blend in with our peers. Some of those kind moments will stay with me forever, and it is with great sadness that now, as an adult, I am unable to express my gratitude for all she did for us. I particularly remember two occasion's, out of many, that Mum went out of her way to support me in my need to blend in. One was while I was at boarding school, and the end of term dance was approaching, like Cinderella, I didn't have a dress to go to the ball. Mum kept promising me she would send one to me, and every day I hoped that a parcel would arrive, but it never did. The day of the dance was nearing, and I was miserable that I had nothing to wear, but to my surprise and happiness, Mum arrived at the boarding school the day before the dance and handed me a parcel with a gorgeous dress inside.

I loved that dress, and I can still see it in all its glory, a dropped waist, blue silk, and very grown-up. The funny thing about all this is that I can't remember ever going to the dance in it, I just remember the agony of having nothing to wear. That's often the way with memories, it seems more natural to recall the sad times that impact your life. The agony of not having a dress to wear seems very trivial to me now. When I had finished my term at boarding school, I went home and hung the dress up in my bedroom wondering when I would be able to wear it again. A few days later I came in from school and went to my bedroom, the first thing I noticed was the dress had gone. I ran down the stairs and yelled at my Mum asking where my dress was, Mum calmly told me she had bought the dress off a neighbour over the road, but she couldn't pay for it, so they had taken it back. I was so despondent about the dress and I'm sure I would not have been happy with my Mum for a long time. I am ashamed to say I didn't make it easy for her, sorry Mum. I can now think of that story with laughter, apart from making Mum feel bad, as it didn't matter, Mum did her best, she never broke her promise, and when I wore the dress, I felt like the belle of the ball. I do feel some guilt towards those childhood responses to growing up, but we all have things we wish we had done differently, things we wish we hadn't done or said but my regret is that I have lost the chance to discuss these matters with my Mum and to thank her for all she tried to do for me. The second occasion was when I met Dave, who Mum liked very much and said he reminded her of my Dad. Dave was smart and immaculate in the way he dressed, and Mum knew I had no real decent clothes to wear when I went out with him. Although Mum didn't have much money, she took me to a shop called Melrose's on Poulton Road and bought me a coat and a couple of dresses which I'm sure would have taken months for her to pay them off. My coat was an imitation fur, which was all the fashion, and I was very grateful to her. I was able to dress nicely now, which gave me more confidence when we went out. I am sure there are many sacrifices Mum made for us all in a quest to provide us with a better life, and I will always be truly grateful to her. After I got married and Dave moved through the ranks to Chief Engineer, I was able to buy some lovely clothes. Fur was in fashion and I had many beautiful fur-trimmed suits, which I purchased from one of the smartest shops in Fleetwood called Stephanie's. How lucky was I?

Mum never remarried, but she did start a relationship with another fisherman and much to our collective horror, he came to live at our house in Heathfield Road. We were all upset about this, and we made life very difficult for Mum by not talking to him. Mum knew how we felt but continued the relationship until he died at sea a decade later. I can reflect on her situation now and realize she would have been really lonely as she was just a young woman. He did bring in a wage that she would have been grateful for, but he was a drinker, and we all hated that. We use to say things like "Dad would not like him" and "how could a Mum do that," which managed to fuel our dislike of him even more. I can't say he was unpleasant to us, but we never gave him a chance, and our feelings towards him never wavered. In the early days, I remember us congregating together, trying to formulate a plan that would expose the fact he was sleeping with Mum. One of us was to walk into the bedroom unannounced and look very surprised and shocked when we discovered he was in bed, although I'm not sure what this would have achieved. Not one of us would volunteer to do it though, and we must have come to the conclusion it would not have changed anything. He died at sea in 1984, and we were in Fleetwood at that time, so I was able to support Mum and go to his funeral. I did feel sorry that Mum had to go through another loss; after all, it wasn't about us. I'm not sure she had ever looked at him as her husband, and I'm not sure she was in love, although he did have a place in her heart. He never took the place of her Jim, my Dad. How naive we all were during those years and how sad we didn't make it easier for Mum. Yet another regret not put right due to the passage of time.

Mum had always been a smoker, and had a cough for as long as I can remember. Mum was diagnosed with lung cancer in 1997, and we were living in NZ at that time with not much money, so I couldn't fly home. My brothers and sisters decided not to tell Mum of her diagnosis, and I'm not sure why they made that decision. I think they thought she would give up. It wouldn't happen these days as the doctor will usually always tell his patient their diagnosis and the expected outcome. I guess in those days, the doctors were more paternalistic and would support a family's wishes. I did respect their decision, after all, I wasn't there, but their decision made it hard for me to communicate with Mum because if I had acted any differently towards her, then she would have known. It turned out Mum had written a letter which they found after her death, and it seems she did know her diagnosis. Mum died in Fleetwood Hospital on the 28th of June 1979 when she was only fifty-five years old. My brother Harry was sailing out of Lowestoft at that time, and the Seaman's Mission helped to get him to Fleetwood so he could be by her side; he managed to get there just before Mum died. I can't say I grieved for my Mum at the time she died, I just wasn't part of it, and somehow it didn't seem real. A few years later we went back to Fleetwood, and it was then that it hit me, no Mum, I was expecting to see her like nothing had changed, but life had changed, and it just wasn't the same without her.

CHAPTER TWELVE

My Teenage years

"It takes courage to grow up and become who you really are."

E. E. Cummings

I MANAGED TO HAVE LOTS of fun in my teenage years, even though I met Dave, and got married when I was only sixteen. I didn't have many best friends apart from my friend Pat from Wingrove Road. We use to go to most places together, and we had lots of fun. Every Saturday, we went to Callaghan's dance studio, where most of our age group went. We would dance to all the latest pop music and follow our boy idols of the time, hoping to get a dance with them. For me, it was easier to get a dance with a boy I liked when they played a progressive dance. The boys had no option but to dance with you and it was the highlight of the night. There were two particular songs we progressively danced to, Sherry by Frankie Valli and the Four Seasons, and Only the Lonely by Roy Orbison, sweet memories!

One night a boy asked if he could walk me home and I had butterflies in my tummy as this was the first time any boy had shown an interest in me. He gave me a kiss goodnight while on our front doorstep. It was my first ever kiss, and I didn't like it, so I spent the next couple of weeks trying to avoid him. During the week (if I was allowed out at night) was spent in coffee bars, and I use to hang out at the Balmoral, Black and White and Morocco cafes. I'm not sure how they made any money as I only ever had enough money for one coffee. I'm sure that the others where in the same boat, but we sat for hours laughing and talking with the crowd. The trendy girls went with their boyfriends to a coffee bar in Cleveleys called the El Cido, and I had the distinction of going there once. There was a boy who I knew liked me, and although I wasn't keen on him in any romantic way, he did ride a motorbike, which was about the only attraction I had to him. One night he asked me if I wanted to go to Cleveleys on the back of his motorbike, and as this was a chance for me to go to the coffee bar, I agreed to go. I knew Mum wouldn't let me go on a motorbike, so I told her I was meeting a girl called Sheila to do our homework together. I got myself ready with such excitement, taking care of my hair as I wanted to make a good impression when we entered the café in Cleveleys. I ditched my school books in a garden at the end of our street, where I had arranged to meet the boy. There was a mixture of excitement and fear at the thought of going on the back of a motorbike. In those days, you didn't wear a crash helmet, so thank goodness nothing happened to me. It was dark by the time I climbed on the back of his bike, and he took off at speed. I think he was showing off because to my horror and fright we did a ton (100mph) down Broadway, one of the main roads, (but it was something I was to boast about later). By the time we got to Cleveleys, I looked like a freak with my carefully back-combed hair standing on end and I felt a bit sick. I didn't get the entrance I desired, in fact nobody even looked up so I didn't do it again. I dropped the poor boy like a ton of bricks and I don't think I ever spoke to him again. Looking back, he was a nice boy, and I can't help but think how shallow I must have been, but I was a teenager after all. I also had a crush on an older boy who lived over the road from us. He would have never looked at me twice because not only was I a kid, but he had a lovely girlfriend who, incidently I liked very much. He worked on the pleasure boats down at the Ferry Beach, so I spent a lot of my time on the beach watching him and dreaming of a future with him, as only a fourteen-year-old would do. I think he knew I had a crush on him as he used to look over and smile at me, which only strengthened and encouraged the dream.

I spent a lot of my time, especially in the summer, on the beach, and as I got older when building sandcastles became tedious, I found another motivation for my love of the beaches. Fleetwood was a seaside resort, and there were many visitors to the area, so there was a chance of striking up friendships, even for a day, with other teenagers, especially boys. It was all very exciting, and I must say innocent because all we did was chat and sometimes have a kiss with a boy. Summer nights were spent around the Boating Lake or on the Mount, and although I never had any money in

**Jennifer outside
Nan's house 1960**

those years, I still had fun. Our activities were innocent, and although there would be a big crowd of us, we never caused any trouble, and we stuck to the rules. The only time I got into trouble was when I went scrumping (pinching apples off trees). There was about five of us I'm not sure how, but the Captain of our youth club found us with a pile of apples. He told us off and said we had to go home straight away or he would tell our parents. In those days you didn't argue and so we went home a little scared and excited at the same time. I felt quite victorious that I had been part of a group that most likely would be talked about the next day, a member of the in-crowd for the first time. I wasn't allowed to go to Blackpool as it was deemed unsafe with the hundreds of visitors that frequented the promenade. Many would come just to get drunk and pick up a girl, so I can't blame Mum for not allowing me to go there. Life was changing for me as I reached fifteen. I wasn't able to stay at school as Mum expected me to start earning a living and I was sad about leaving school. I would have loved to stay on but on the other hand I was excited, at long last I would have some money of my own.

I am so happy I grew up in the 1960's and have the memories I have. One of the biggest, defining aspects of that time was the music. Although rock and roll began affecting Britain in the 1950s, it wasn't until the early sixties and the emergence of groups like the Beatles, that music truly began its revolutionary changes. I loved the Beatles, and of course, now they remind me of meeting Dave and us both listening to their songs together. We use to lie on the settee at Mum's house and listen to Radio Luxemburg into the early hours of the morning, often falling asleep. I would wake up in a panic, scared about what Mum would say. Dave would have to walk home to his house in Shakespeare Road, and I was glad when we finally got married because he wouldn't have to walk home alone again. We didn't like to be apart, we only had two or three days together before he went back to sea, so we made the most of those days. I guess mum had an idea of what it was like to have such a short time together so she left us alone. When I left school, I went to work at Mullards, which manufactured valves for television and radios. Mullards was one of the largest employers in Fleetwood, and I was lucky to get a job there. I did "piecework" which I was good at and I could work quickly and accurately. I got a good wage but had to give it all to Mum, who gave me money back to spend on myself. I can remember feeling exhausted when I first started work and spent most of the weekends asleep in bed, only getting up for meals. I left Mullards and went to work in a grocery shop down Lord Street. I'm not sure of the reason why, but I liked it there and loved measuring out cheese and butter and weighing the sugar and biscuits. Most of the food came in bulk and had to be measured accurately for obvious reason. The butter and cheese came in big blocks and again you had to be careful when you cut it as it could result in wastage. Mum did a big order of food to be delivered while I was working there, but she didn't pay for it. The owner stopped my wages and I ended up having to pay it off, which took many weeks. By this stage, I was going out with Dave, and he use to give me money for nylon stockings and any toiletries I needed, he was indeed my soul mate, even then. I eventually left the grocery shop, and ended up back at Mullards, and that is where I stayed until I was married a few months later.

Many people have asked me if I regretted being married so young and missing out on my teenage years, but I didn't have any regrets. It was the path I chose to take, and I loved Dave with all my heart. I felt safe with him and certainly did not want to live my life without him. I still have happy memories of the days with my friends, and the times we shared, even though they were short. I am sure I will always have many tales to tell of my teenage years, but they are stored somewhere in my brain where only glimpses of memories are released.

Life wasn't all bad, and I don't want to give that impression, Mum tried hard to make our lives fun and happy despite the lack of funds. One year she decided to take the three eldest girls on holiday to Salisbury to see Stonehenge. We set off in the car but hadn't got very far when the police stopped us because we had no car registration. Amazingly the policeman let Mum off, and we all thought it was because of her histrionics. Mum put on her best act and the policeman listened with patience to her arguments about it being our "first holiday together "and it was "unfair to stop us" and "go and catch the real criminals". The policeman was excellent and allowed us to travel to Preston to get the car registered before we set off, and looking back, I think Mum was lucky to have got away without a fine. We did have a lovely time though and stayed in some delightful old inns which must have cost Mum quite a bit of money, I think we were away for about five days, and it is the only time I can remember being on holiday with her.

CHAPTER THIRTEEN

A Memorable 21ˢᵗ Birthday Party

"In all the world, there is no heart for me like yours. In all the world, there is no love for you like mine"

Maya Angelou

I DIDN'T HAVE ANY REAL boyfriends before I met Dave but I had lots of crushes on boys who didn't even realize I existed. I look back at my very few single years with happiness as I did have a good time and have no regrets about those years being cut short. As a teenager, I always dreamt of meeting Prince Charming and being swept away to live a life of love and devotion. I met Dave when I was fifteen and I remember it well. Patricia, my sister, was dating a fisherman who was sailing on the same ship as Dave, and although I don't think they were particularly good friends, they were shipmates. It was her boyfriend's twenty-first birthday, and Mum allowed Tricia to have a party for him at our house. I will never forget that day and I know my family has heard this story before. I use to come home from work every day for lunch, and on this particular day, a boy was standing at the gate chatting with Trish's boyfriend. I went inside and asked Mum who he was, and she told me his name but also that he was engaged. Dave had a grey suit on, white shirt and white socks, which looked very smart, but I did notice his shoes had round toes, which were definitely not in fashion, and when you are fifteen, those sorts of detail are crucial. That night he arrived at the party with his fiancé and although Dave and I didn't talk we kept glancing at each other. I don't think it was love at first sight, but there was a definite attraction between us both. Later in the evening, I went into the kitchen to get a drink, and Dave was there talking to someone, he came over and put his arms around me, and we kissed. We chatted together till the end of the night, and I thought no more about it. The next morning when I got up for work, there was a tap on the front door, and to my surprise it was Dave wanting to walk me to work. He was going to sea later that morning and he wanted to ask if we could see each other again. I told him that I wouldn't see him while he was engaged and that was the end of it as far as I was concerned. I didn't expect to see him again so I said goodbye and never gave him another thought. Two weeks later, to my surprise, he was waiting for me outside work and told me he was free to go out with me and would I go out with him. The rest is history as they say. We had a short dating time, much like my teenage years, I guess. We met in September 1963 and spent some happy times together. Life took me on a new course, and I started to experience a very different way of life. I had never been to a pub before, and although I was underage, I was never challenged when I was with Dave. It was a whole new world to me, going around in taxi's, meeting Dave's shipmates, and generally having a good time. We always went to a record shop on Poulton Road when he was in from sea and we huddled together in a small booth listening to records he wanted to buy. We sometimes went to Blackpool on nights out, which is definitely something I hadn't done before, and I was loving my life with Dave. I really liked Dave's mum Edith and got on well with her, they had a lovely house in Shakespeare Road, and I was always made welcome. When I got pregnant, Dave's mum and dad were not happy as I was only sixteen and they were concerned we were both too young to get married even though Dave was twenty, they thought it wouldn't last. If only they could see us now, married for fifty-six years with three adult children and three gorgeous grandchildren, not to mention my lovely daughter and sons-in-laws.

Our wedding day 1964

We got married on the 8th July 1964, I was about six weeks pregnant, and although being pregnant was frowned upon, we were happy and in love. Reverend Milner married us at St Pauls Church on a Wednesday, which was an unusual day to get married as most couples got married on a Saturday. Having a Special Licence allowed us to give Reverend Milner short notice as we couldn't choose an exact date with Dave being at sea. We could not afford for Dave to take a trip off to plan a future wedding date so a Special Licence was the next best thing. We had a lovely wedding followed by a reception at Healds Café, which was a popular choice for many brides in the 1960's. I would have loved Dad to walk me down the aisle; it's every girl's dream, but one of his good friends, Stan Birch also a fisherman, did the job well. In the space of three years, not only did he give me away, but he also gave my sisters Janet and Patricia away. He was kept very busy being a stand-in Dad for the Gorst girls and I know Dad would have been grateful to him. I was about six weeks pregnant when I got married and I had terrible morning sickness. I was worried about getting ready inbetween being sick but I did manage to get through the excitement of my wedding morning and by the time I got to the church, I was feeling very much like a beautiful bride. I had to go around the block in the wedding car a couple of times as unknown to me Dave had left the church as he wanted to use the toilet! I floated down the aisle with butterflies in my tummy, expecting my Prince Charming to turn around and tell me how beautiful I looked. Instead, he turned to look at me and whispered that his brother and wife had arrived unexpectantly from Portsmouth. That anti-climax was something I have never let Dave forget to this day. His brother Ken and his wife Jean had travelled especially to be at the wedding, and although it was lovely to see them and such a surprise, I didn't expect those words from Dave. I had borrowed my head-dress from Janet, and then Tricia wore it for her wedding the following year. The next day my red roses bouquet was kindly taken by one of the trawlers to drop into the sea over where my Dad was lost. We spent our honeymoon, two days, at "Ourgate," which was jokingly Sam and Edith's house in Shakespeare Road. The two days we had together went too quickly and I cried when Dave went back to sea. I realized I had started the life my Mum had experienced, and I didn't like it at all.

Edith and Sam made me welcome in their home, which was lovely and cosy and I was able to buy a new bed and a few things for our small bedroom before Dave came in from sea again. My wage from Dave was £10 a week, and I thought it was a fortune, I walked around Woolworths, thinking I could buy anything I wanted, but I bought nothing. When Dave was in from sea, we used the parlour (now called the front room) as our own room. It had Dave's new radiogram in it, which he was very proud of, so we played records, kissed, and talked about what it would be like to be a Mum and Dad. Edith and Sam were very generous, allowing my friend Pat to visit any time, and most evenings, my brother Jimmy would come around to sit with me. Although I was quite happy in their home, I longed for a place of our own, somewhere that just belonged to us. I decided after a couple of months to look for a flat, and it didn't take me long before I found an upstairs flat in Harris Street. The landlady was called Mrs Oldfield, and she was a lovely lady who was helpful and friendly. It was a fully furnished flat, and I stayed there till I was due to have the baby. No one wanted me to be alone as the baby's birthdate got nearer, so we left the flat and went back to Sam and Edith's before Christmas. We had some happy times in that flat and Pat, my friend, stayed most nights when Dave was at sea. Pat and I use to sleep in the big double bed and talk about the arrival of the new baby, and she would talk about her boyfriend.

I remember the Christmas of 1964 when I had moved out of the flat; Mum wanted me at home for Christmas Day, and Dave was at sea. I went to her house on Christmas Eve day, and it was such fun to be back with the family as we prepared for Christmas Day. As usual in our house, there was a huge real Christmas tree beautifully decorated with baubles, tinsel, and chocolates, and there was a lot of excitement as we laughed and chatted with each other. We were all older, so the excitement was no longer for the arrival of Father Christmas, it was for the magical atmosphere which Mum and Dad had created each Christmas from when we were all firstborn. At this stage, I was nearly at the end of my pregnancy, and I was feeling very uncomfortable, Dave was at sea, so the light-hearted banter of the family was a welcome relief as I missed him so much. I made mince pies and helped prepare the Christmas dinner, but I must have done too much as I had backache for most of Christmas Day, leaving everyone anxious that I was in labour. I felt sad that Dave had missed our first Christmas together, but he did send me a telegram to say how much he was missing me and I had filled his seabag with chocolates and presents, hoping he would have a reasonable Christmas Day without me. It was the first time but not the last time we spent many special occasions apart, including the birth of our daughters Trudy and Sam.

CHAPTER FOURTEEN

A Young Mum

"Having kids-the responsibility of rearing good, kind, ethical, responsible human beings is the biggest job anyone can embark on"

Maria Shriver

MY BABY WAS DUE ON 15ᵗʰ January, two days after my seventeenth birthday, but that date came and went. Dave was due back at sea on that date and I was hoping it would happen before he went back, but no such luck. We had bought a bassinet for the baby and had everything prepared, my crowning glory being the pram. It was a top of the range Silver Cross pram which had a brown cover and hood and on the side was a curve of decorated flowers. The Silver Cross shop was on Poulton Road, and they let you pay weekly for the pram and would store it till it was needed. They did a roaring trade in Fleetwood, and most of the babies in that era were transported around town as if they were Royalty. I bought viyella nightgowns, which was a fabric made from a twilled mixture of cotton and wool (only the best for my baby). They were very expensive but were quite plain so I embroidered a green leafy pattern on them. In those days, you kept a newborn in nighties for the first six weeks, and I wanted them to be a little bit more colourful till I could dress her in the beautiful clothes I had bought and those that were gifts. I followed the traditions in play at the time listening to the advice from my Mum and Edith; after all, I had just had my seventeenth birthday. I adapted well and had a feel for what I needed to do, and felt quite confident as I waited for my baby to be born. Everything had gone well during my pregnancy apart from the initial morning sickness, and I had no health issues at all, so I expected that the birth would be without any complications. On the evening of the 31st January, my friend Pat had come to sit with me, and at about 10 pm I started to have some back pain, I never said anything as it was not unusual for me to have this type of pain. Edith and Sam had gone to bed, and Pat left for home about 11 pm. The back pain continued for one or two hours and about 1 am I realised I was clutching the back of a chair, so I thought maybe this was it, perhaps I was in labour. Excited that I would soon have my baby but scared to death about how it was to come out, I woke Sam and Edith. Not everyone had cars and telephones, so Sam got on his pushbike and rode to the telephone box at Manor Road to call an ambulance. I had booked into Milton Lodge many months before, and my packed case had been ready to go for about a month. The ambulance arrived, and I climbed into it, taking a ride that would change me from a young girl to a mother, and all the responsibilities this entailed.

When I arrived at Milton Lodge, an amiable nurse admitted me and put me into a bed, saying she would be in and out to check on me. I was so scared, and the pains were increasing, but I never made a sound, I was too busy listening to a lady screaming and shouting which scared me even more. Once the lady had gone quiet, and I presumed had given birth, the nurse came into the room to check on me. She told me the baby was well on the way and moved me to another place, the labour room, which is where I had my gorgeous baby girl. The midwife told me I had done well, and I heard her say to the other nurse it was not unusual for girls of my age to go through labour and delivery without making any noise. I was so delighted, a baby girl who was born at 6.30 am and weighed 6lb 10oz. I couldn't believe it; I was a mother! Everyone was thrilled I had a girl, particularly Edith and Sam. My brother Harry thought she was perfect because she was born on his birthday, and he was always proud of that fact. I could not believe I had a baby girl, my baby had arrived at last. I found it hard to eat that day because I was so excited. Sam sent Dave a telegram to tell him he was a dad, and I knew he would be so proud. We had decided on a girl's name before she was born and I liked the name Trudy only because a girl in my class at school had that name and I thought it was unusual. My euphoria only lasted a couple of days as Trudy contracted an eye infection and had to be transferred to Devonshire Road Isolation Hospital near Blackpool. I was devastated and wanted to go with her, but the doctor wouldn't let me leave Milton Lodge as he thought I would just want to travel from home each day to visit her, which he deemed to be too much for me. In those days, there was no facility for mothers to stay with their children, unbelievable, I know. I resigned myself to stay for a few more days, but watching the other mothers cuddling their babies was too much for me, and I cried myself to sleep each night. I felt very alone without Dave; although he had sent me a telegram and lovely flowers, it just added to my misery, sorry Dave.

Eventually, they let me leave the hospital, and a friend of Sam and Edith's kindly took me to the hospital each day in his car. Dave was still at sea, while my world seemed to be falling apart, but Trudy was improving and I was told she would be home soon, and I couldn't wait. The first thing I did was go and collect my upmarket pram and push it back home. When I saw anyone I knew, they would stop me to look at the baby, but of course, there was no baby in the pram, and I had to explain all the events of her first few days to each one of them. When I finally went to collect her from the hospital, I was so happy, at last, I was going to be able to look after her and be a mother. I chose one of my many matinee jackets with a matching bonnet and a beautiful shawl to wrap her in, and she looked gorgeous. Dave came home a few days later, after experiencing a rough trip with terrible weather. At one stage, the trawler had gone on its side, and he thought it would be lost and he would never even get to see his baby daughter.

I was so excited about his homecoming; he was due home about 9pm and I couldn't wait to see his face when he met his daughter for the first time. I envisaged Dave looking at his beautiful baby daughter with pride as she slept in her carrycot, then glancing at me with so much love in his eyes. (I was such a romantic) I started setting the scene to get the result I dreamed of. I gave Trudy a feed, put her in the carrycot, and dimmed the lights in our front room. I waited with anticipation for the knock on the door and Dave arrived home at about 10 pm, an hour later than I expected. But there was no tranquil, romantic scene as he walked through the door. Trudy had woken up for a feed and was screaming at the top of her lungs, and I was very flustered. Poor Dave must have wondered what was going on. But this was a snapshot of real life, caught in a moment of time when my romantic dream was lost forever. Perhaps the moment was not so imperfect though, at least it gave Dave chance to experience the reality of having a baby in the house straight away.

I can't say it was easy to have a newborn baby, and I had a lot to learn, but I was comfortable with her and did what I felt was right. I had my Mum and Dave's mum Edith around, so this gave me confidence. Trudy was a good baby and the only problem I had was feeding her. I didn't want to breastfeed, and although I have regrets about that now, I was just too young to understand the benefits at that time. Routine was important in those days, and it was usual to feed the baby every three to four hours. Trudy was so slow to feed, and by the time she finished one bottle, it was time for her to have another one, so I had very little time in between. I was very proud of her as she was a gorgeous baby, and all the family loved her. Everyone wanted to look at her when we were out walking, and it took an age to do any shopping down our main street. Trudy did eventually settle into a routine, and life with a new baby became a little easier.

Trudy at six months old

CHAPTER FIFTEEN

Our First Real Home

"As corny as it sounds, to me, home is where the heart is.... So moving houses is just another way in which I get to experience life"

Ellen DeGeneres

WHEN TRUDY WAS A FEW months old, George and Janet gave us a wonderful gift, a chance to own our own home. There was a company building some new houses at the top of Grange Road, and you only needed a small deposit; they cost £2400 in 1965, and George gave us £50 for the deposit. I was only eighteen and Dave was twenty-two, so it was an excellent opportunity for us and so generous of George, it was a lot of money in those days. We were very excited as we watched the house being built and by the time the house was finished, we had managed to save for a new fitted carpet, a lounge suite, and our solicitor fees. Some of the furniture was second-hand, and although mismatched, I thought our house looked fantastic. It was the first time I had been on my own with Trudy, but I managed well. My brother Jimmy often came to stay and keep me company, which helped me a great deal especially having a little one to look after. The house was at the top of Grange Road, which had open fields, and it was very blustery in the winter, which made it quite hard to push the pram sometimes, but I managed to walk into town a few days a week which kept me fit. We hadn't been in the house very long when I became pregnant with Sam, so with the inevitable morning sickness and managing Trudy, life became just a tad bit harder. We got a telephone installed because I was on my own and this was considered very posh. Not many people had telephones and neighbours would come and ask if they could use the phone, which at times was a nuisance. It was also costly as we had to pay for each call. I didn't want to stop them using the phone and in the end, I placed a coin box next to the telephone so they put the cost of the telephone call into the box, which worked very well.

Dave was unable to have a trip off so he went to sea a couple of days before the baby was due. I went to stay at Sam and Edith's house, which would make it easier for me if I went into labour, and for Trudy to be looked after while I was in the hospital. I missed my house and Dave, but it was nice to have some company as the nights were long in December. In the early hours of the morning on the 31st December 1966, my water broke, and I went into labour. This time I had to go to Blackpool Victoria Hospital, which was ten miles away as Milton Lodge was closed for deliveries. I was happy that I would be transferred back to Milton Lodge after the birth, though, and thankful the

Jennifer age 18 after moving into their new home1966

family would be nearer. When I arrived at the hospital, it was hectic, and I knew I was not a welcome sight because the nurse ignored me and left me sitting in a very uncomfortable wheelchair. Eventually they put me into a post-natal room with about five other women who had all given birth to their babies.

I laboured on throughout the morning until I felt I wanted to push and I asked one of the mothers to call for a nurse. The nurse eventually came bustling in, pulled the covers back and told me I was nowhere near ready and she left the room. I was horrified and didn't know what to do, but I knew I was ready to push. I had no other choice but to ask the now anxious new mother to find me another nurse, "but not the one who had just been in" I said. It was awful, and I'm sure it upset the other patients; however, another nurse came in, pulled the covers off me again, and said, "Oh my God," then called for help. They started to push me to the labour ward, but I didn't make it, and so I ended up in a linen room on the way. That is where I had my baby girl Samantha who arrived at 1230pm; there was no apology, no sympathy, just nothing from them about the treatment I had received. The nurses had left me alone again just after I had Samantha. I felt like I wanted to vomit but there was nothing to be sick into, all I could do was to lean over the side of the bed and vomit all over the floor. I'm sure this didn't help my reputation with the nurses and I don't know how I managed to come out of the birthing event unscathed. Those nurses were lucky that nothing went wrong with the delivery or my baby and I have never forgotten how they made me feel. I knew they were busy, but there was no excuse for their lack of professionalism and care. This sort of treatment lasted throughout my stay, which thank goodness was only for twenty-four hours. I even had to fight when they brought my baby for me to feed. I politely asked the nurse for a bottle to feed her with, and the nurse looked at me as if I was crazy and said there are no bottles, you will have to breastfeed. I was only 18, and I hadn't changed my mind about breastfeeding, but the nurse was insistent. In the end, I just held my ground and refused to breastfeed but the nurse was unmoved and ended up bringing me a jug of milk and a spoon to feed her, which I did until I got back to Milton Lodge. By the time I got back, my baby did not know how to suck, and the nurses were very annoyed when I told them of the treatment I had received. To top it off, I ended up being very unwell and I was put into isolation at Milton Lodge because of a strep throat. When Dave came in from sea, I was still in hospital feeling really sorry for myself. The ship arrived home in the early evening and he came straight to Milton Lodge to see me. It was around 9pm and although visiting time was over, they kindly let him in to see me. I was so pleased to see him and he made me feel better straight away. I went home the next day and it was wonderful to be back in my own home with my babies and their dad. Now fifty-four years later Blackpool Victoria Hospital has got an excellent obstetric unit, where mothers and babies have the best of care so maybe I was one of the pioneers in its progress.

I think I managed well with a toddler and a new baby, the house was perfect for us, and I loved it. The only problem was that we only had a coal fire that heated the downstairs, but it was always cold upstairs, and I had to put mittens and hats on the girls to keep them warm. We eventually had central heating installed, which was very welcomed and saved me lighting a fire, and the girls were kept warm. I didn't like the nights alone, and one night when Dave was at sea, I heard a strange noise and was frightened something, or someone was in the bedroom. The sound turned out to be a mouse dragging a biscuit down the hole where the new radiator was. Everyone who knows me can imagine how this sent me into an absolute panic, but I saw the night out, without any sleep I may add. The next morning, I packed up everything we needed and headed to Edith and Sam's. Sam caught the mouse the next day, and we never saw it again, but I stayed with them until Dave came in from sea. Just in case! We had some happy times in this house, including my twenty-first birthday and I often wonder would we still have lived there had it not been sold to emigrate to New Zealand in 1969.

CHAPTER SIXTEEN

New Zealand

"Change can be scary, but you know what's scarier? Allowing
<u>fear</u> to stop you from growing, evolving, and progressing"
Mandy Hale

DAVE AND I HAD OFTEN talked about leaving Fleetwood and wanting a better life for our children. I hated Dave going to sea and could not bear the thought that one day he might never return just as my Dad hadn't. In the 1960s, many people were emigrating mainly to Australia, and I remember talking to a lady who was leaving the following week. She spoke of a new life with better opportunities, beaches, and sunshine, and when I told Dave we became hooked on the idea. None of us know what the future holds for us, and the idea of a new beginning in a new country was a bit scary, but we were optimistic about starting a fresh and new life away from Fleetwood. We really wanted to go to New Zealand because it was supposed to be a lot more English than Australia, and we thought it would be easier for us to assimilate in a similar country. We applied to New Zealand House but our application was rejected as Dave's trade was not on the needed list. We were a little bit disappointed but there was always Australia. The process of emigrating to Australia was a lot easier and people were encouraged to apply. It was at a time when a lot of British people were choosing to migrate, and the criteria and process, although had many elements to it, was quick and straightforward. After an interview, and a medical assessment, we were accepted. We were given a leaving date and we were given the name of the ship which was taking us to our new life. We packed all our furniture and belongings and they were put into storage until needed in Australia; we were all ready for our new adventure. Although apprehensive, we were excited too, but I don't think I had realized what an emotional parting with my family would be like, and in the end, it was just awful. We had planned to go to Adelaide, and stay in a complex owned by a building firm. This Company would then build us a house and we just about had enough money to do this. They sent us pictures of the house which was a bungalow with four bedrooms and two bathrooms and I felt like we would be living in a mansion.

In the meantime, Dave was still going to sea and was a Chief Engineer, he had done exceptionally well, and I believe he was one of the youngest Chief Engineers at that time to sail from Fleetwood. After we had received our sailing date to Australia, he came in from sea to discover the firm he worked for, Boston Deep Sea Fisheries, was leasing a trawler to a New Zealand company, and they needed a crew. The *Boston Seafire* was to sail to Nelson in New Zealand. We were in quite a dilemma as we still preferred to go to New Zealand and this left us with a tough decision. We thought the Australian Government wouldn't be happy if we decided not to go but when we did decide to cancel, much to my surprise, they were quite understanding about our situation and wished us all the best. I now know they must have encountered many couples who had changed their mind; after all, it was a massive decision to emigrate in the first place. Dave had applied to be a crew member and was successful in gaining a position as an engineer, and we were over the moon to be going to New Zealand, our first choice. We had to change all of our plans and get our furniture back, which was loaded into the *Boston Seafire's* fish room for the six-week journey. The ship sailed for New Zealand in September 1969. We all waved the trawler goodbye from the Ferry Beach just as we had done so many times before. Dave and I had not been apart for that long before, and although it was sad, I knew we had made the right choice for us as a family. The girls and I stayed with Mum until Dave was ready for us to join him. It had taken the *Boston Seafire* six weeks to get to Nelson, but he just wanted to make sure the company he was working for was okay. They had unloaded and stored our furniture into the factory, but it had been damaged. Most of our belongings had taken a beating on the passage over, so we didn't have that many possessions left to set up house. I left England to join Dave in December 1969 with our two girls aged four and three. It was sad to be leaving the family, my Mum had got used to having us at home, and my brother Jimmy had a real bond with the girls and was very upset to say goodbye to them. I couldn't wait to see Dave, but I knew he would be at sea when we arrived. It was arranged for a relative of Sam and Edith's next-door neighbour to meet us and they kindly let us stay with them till we found a place to live.

It was such a long journey on my own, but the girls were good. Other passengers would read a book to them or they would crayon with them, which helped me out because the girls never went to sleep at the same time. By the time I arrived in Auckland, I was exhausted, and the air hostess took the girls around the airport to give me a break while I waited for our flight to Nelson. I had completely lost my bearings after having stopped in Honolulu and Fiji and was dreading another long haul, but of course, it was only a short trip from Auckland to Nelson, which I hadn't realized. I noticed the New Zealand flight felt entirely different compared to the British flight, it felt more relaxed with the gentle Pacific music playing, and the air hostesses appeared to be friendlier; I hoped this was a sign of a welcoming New Zealand. By the time we reached Nelson we must have looked a sight, tiredness had crept up to the girls, and Trudy was tearful, Sam was clingy, and I looked like a wreck. It was hot, and the sun hurt our eyes, but the welcome committee did an excellent job of recognizing the situation and took care of all our needs. There were two couples at the airport all from Fleetwood, and they became good friends to us. It was wonderful to see Dave again as I had missed him, he seemed to be happy and settled but I found the routine of the boat was awful. They went to sea for either one or two weeks and Dave even as the engineer had to help land the fish when they came in. He then had to wait around for his money. He had no real-time at home, often returning to sea after a day, which was worse than being back in Fleetwood. We had to start making a life for ourselves and eventually settled in Richmond, Nelson. We had a lovely old flat with nice young neighbours who had children about the same age as ours. Our furniture, although damaged, was still usable and didn't look too bad in our comfortable little home. After about a year, Dave decided to leave the ship as it was no life for us, and I was homesick. The girls hardly saw Dave, and I never got a break from them at all, but the young family next door gave me as much support as they could. Dave managed to get a job servicing trucks and he did the 3pm-11pm shift, it wasn't great hours but at least he was home every day.

Joan, who had met us at the airport, was a head nurse at Nelson Hospital, and I had told her I wanted to try nursing when the girls were older, and she very kindly arranged for me to be a nurse aid at Nelson Hospital doing two nightshifts a week. I thought this would be good for me to meet other people and to earn some extra money. I got measured for a white uniform, a white cap and a red cape that fitted snugly around my shoulders. I was looking forward to my first shift and I certainly looked like a nurse even though I had never worked in a hospital before. I had to get a taxi to work as I couldn't drive, and the hospital was about 20 minutes from our home. When I arrived they gave me a locker, and I wrapped my purse in a scarf, placing it inside. I never gave the security of my purse a second thought as I was nervous and eager to get to the ward. I was greeted by a Registered Nurse who I was to work with. The nurse showed me around the ward, pointing out the sluice room and a treatment room. I followed her like a puppy, and it all seemed to be fine when the lights were on, but once they went off, the place felt quite different. Around 0300, the RN told me she was going for her break and said to me if there were any problems to phone the Night Supervisor. I was left sitting at a desk feeling very scared in my new surroundings. After about ten minutes just as I had got used to the noises around me, I heard a voice shouting "nurse, nurse" in a loud booming voice, and my heart started to pound. I just sat there, not knowing what to do, thinking he would soon go back to sleep, but he kept calling. By this stage, I was at my wit's end, and I hadn't a clue what to do so I called the night supervisor, I told her someone was calling out and wanted a nurse, but she had gone on her break. The supervisor, bless her, didn't say anything other than I will be there soon. I waited until she arrived to be rescued from my situation and by that time, I was near to tears as the man was still calling, and his voice sounded angrier. The night supervisor took complete charge and told me very quietly that I was the nurse, which was a massive surprise to me. Taking me under her wing, we went to the patient's room to see what he wanted, and to my amazement, I didn't see a bad-tempered man but an older sweet looking gentleman who only wanted to wee. The night supervisor showed me where to get a bottle from and helped the patient with it, she never sounded cross with me, and I was thankful for that. I am sure that story got told many times by the supervisor who must have found it so funny, especially with the look on my face as she pronounced me as being a nurse, and it is certainly one I will never forget. I did manage to get through the night but was so tired the next morning. I was not feeling too good about the patient incident and I was looking forward to going home. When I got to the locker, to my horror, I discovered my purse was gone. The taxi had been pre-ordered, and I didn't know what to do. I went out and told him about my purse and that I would have to cancel him; however, I had no idea how I was going to get home. He was very kind and cheerful, which is exactly what I needed at that moment. He told me not to worry and to hop in the cab and he would take me home. I offered to give him the fare when I arrived home, but he wouldn't take it from me, and I never forgot his kindness. The next night I felt a little more relaxed and useful, the patients didn't scare me quite as much and I was feeling a little bit like a nurse. The next episode that sent me into a spin was when a patient died. I had never seen a dead person before, which was bad enough, but when I had to help with the last offices, it was the last straw. I saw the shift through to the next morning but I knew my Florence Nightingale shifts, all two of them, were over. I contacted Joan and told her nursing wasn't for me, so she got me a job in the kitchen, which I loved, felt useful, made some friends, and earned a bit of extra money, precisely what I wanted to do in the first place.

My homesickness continued even though I was adapting to our new life, but it was hard with Dave working in the evenings. The girls would be in bed and I felt lonely. I couldn't phone my Mum as we didn't have a phone and even if we did have one, we couldn't afford to pay for a call to England, so there was only letter writing. In the end, Dave decided to apply for a job in Christchurch, and he was successful. We had managed to save up $500 to buy an old car, and we were so proud of it, Dave had driven it from the sellers, but he didn't have a driving license which he had to have before we could drive to Christchurch. What an adventure it was for us, we hadn't been outside of Nelson and we were looking forward to the journey. Dave had managed to get a lovely fully furnished house to rent in Opawa in Christchurch and we were able to sell the few possessions we had, which gave us a little extra money to help with the move. The girls were excited about moving, and so we packed up the car and left Nelson with our two little girls, not knowing what the future would hold for us. It took us all day to travel to Christchurch, and the journey was breathtaking, it was the first time we had experienced the scenery New Zealand had to offer. We drove over the Lewis Pass, and Dave did a perfect job of driving all the way without any problems. When we arrived, we stayed in a motel for two nights. We were able to meet the couple who had rented the house to us before they left for their trip to England. They made us very welcome and liked the idea that a little family was going to care for their home, they were such a lovely couple. The house was a two-storied property with a gorgeous garden, and we were thrilled to be there. We settled into our lives quite comfortably and life seemed to be looking up for us at last. Dave was working normal hours, Trudy was at the local school, and Sam went to a kindergarten which was close by.

CHAPTER SEVENTEEN

A New Beginning....Again

*"Keep on beginning and failing. Each time you fail, start all over
again, and you will grow stronger until you have accomplished
a purpose – not the one you began with perhaps, but one you'll
be glad to remember"*

Anne Sullivan

WE QUITE LOVED CHRISTCHURCH, IT was such a beautiful city,
and the people were friendly. I always think of Christchurch and not
Nelson as the point where we started to feel at home. I was still homesick
for Fleetwood, but as I got busier, this seemed to lessen, and I began to
enjoy our very different way of life. Despite my misgivings about being
a nurse, it seems destiny kept placing me on that pathway, so I started to
stroll along with it. There were not too many jobs that I could do at the
weekends, which didn't involve nursing of some description. I needed to
work at the weekends so that Dave could look after the girls as there was
no one else to help us. It was our only option, we didn't know a soul. Dave
started to enjoy the parent role, it was the first time he had to look after
the girls for any length of time, and they, in turn, enjoyed having their dad
around. He did things differently to me in regards to what they had for
lunch and dinner, and my adult children still talk about those meals. He
was a dab-hand at cooking rice risotto from a packet, and on a Sunday, he
made a party-like dinner which consisted of sandwiches, jelly, ice-cream,

biscuits, crackers and cheese and potato chips. They were allowed to eat the food in any order, and they truly loved those Sunday dinners, how our lives had changed. To this day, my grandchildren love what they call "grandads' dinner "and will choose it above any other food when we get together.

With much trepidation, I applied for a job as a nurse-aid in a geriatric hospital, which was not too far away. I did not want to do nights as the ghost that followed me from Nelson Hospital was still hovering on my shoulder and I thought I could manage day duty without being too spooked. The hospital was called Coronation Hospital, and it was lovely. It had three floors and had been the main tuberculosis hospital for Christchurch. The Sisters were the only Registered nurses, and one was in charge of each shift and each level. The Sisters did the medications and dressings, and the nurse-aids did all the personal care which I may add, was hard work. The Matron was a delightful lady who we all respected; she had the knack of being friendly in a most professional way that maintained the respect we had for her. Matron knew us all and always stopped to chat and ask about our families; she had a daughter that worked with us as a nurse-aid in the holidays. Dianne was lots of fun, and she often looked dishevelled in her uniform; often getting into trouble from her mother for looking unprofessional. We never worried about her being the Matron's daughter; we all liked working with her. She brightened up our shift, and we laughed at her antics. The Sisters in those days were respected, and you didn't dare do anything wrong. They issued the orders, and by golly, we had to follow them. If we were sat in the office when Matron walked in, we had to stand up and put our hands behind our backs till she gave us permission to sit down again. I never minded doing this because we did respect her and the Sisters, and it was the nursing etiquette back then. It is here that I fell in love with nursing, it was such hard work, but I learned so much and soon became a trusted member of staff with a reputation for giving excellent care. It was also where we made our friends, and we soon started to have a social life although sometimes it was hard to do with working every weekend. We were, however, all in the same boat, as most of us only worked at the weekends, so we arranged our social life around our shifts. Two of the nurses became my best friends, and we were lucky because our husbands also got on well together, as did our children. Another friend worked in the kitchen as a cook and we started to have dinner at their house, her husband was a nice chap and we also became their friends, seeing them often. Those times were in the era when you had dinner parties to entertain your friends, and we all took turns, I learned many recipes and tips from my friends during those times especially my friend from the kitchen who was an excellent cook.

Our years in Christchurch were happy ones, the girls were growing up, and we managed to save and buy a house again. The house was in St John's Street, Linwood, and we were happy to have our own place again. I had only been working at the hospital for a few months when I discovered I was pregnant, unexpected, but great news for us. The girls were getting older, and our incomes were good, so it was a good time for us to expand our family. Although I had terrible morning sickness, I worked till I was six months pregnant and then went back to work when the baby was six weeks old. I didn't have a choice really as we needed the money and I missed my friends from work. At the end of my pregnancy, I was what you would say "very large." I was two weeks overdue and feeling very tired and irritable. One night we were having dinner, and it came on the news about a lady having quintuplets. Sam, even at age four, being very forthright, wanted to know how the lady could have so many babies in her tummy when I only had one and "look how big you are mummy," but I must admit I was rather large and very uncomfortable. Obstetric care was different in the early 1970's, there were no scans, and midwives monitored you at an ante-natal clinic. If all was going well, you only saw your GP at specific points throughout the pregnancy. I was under the care of the Christchurch Woman's Hospital. At the end of a long two weeks of being overdue, they admitted me for an induction as there was no sign the baby would come on its own. For the first time, Dave was home, and I was looking forward to having some support through my labour. He was working for Skyline Garages as a supervisor, so was able to stay with me throughout the induction and labour. He was still not allowed to be present for the birth, and we had to part when I went into the delivery room, which was just awful. He was ushered to the waiting room to sit with the other impending fathers waiting nervously for news. I had David at 5.30 pm, a big boy weighing 9lb 1oz with broad shoulders and the most fantastic mop of golden hair, yes golden, not red. Dave told me the nurse shouted down the corridor to him that he had a little All Black, and Dave said he could not believe he had a son. We were all thrilled to have a boy, and the girls loved to help me look after him, it felt different somehow having Dave around with a new baby, and I felt much more relaxed as a new mother again. Another exciting event in those years was to have my sister Margaret emigrate to NZ, she arrived in December 1970, just a year after we arrived. It was lovely to have her in our lives as I had missed my sisters. Marg got a job working in the kitchen at the hospital where I worked, and she quickly made lots of friends. The children loved their Aunty Marg, and she spoilt them all, she was a great help with David and lived with us till she got married.

In 1974 we decided we wanted to go home for a while as I still had periods of being homesick but certainly not like I had when we first left Fleetwood. I wanted Mum to see the children again, and it was an excellent opportunity to reconnect the girls to their English family. It was also a chance for my family to meet David, something I know Mum was longing to do. Marg was settled and had got married so they decided to rent the house from us. It gave us an excellent opportunity to leave at this time, and I knew Marg would look after our house. Although I did miss home, we didn't want to live in Fleetwood again, so leaving the house cared for was important to me. We spent a year in Fleetwood, where we enjoyed catching up with friends and visiting our old haunts. We made the most of the time we had in Fleetwood, but we missed our life in New Zealand and was very happy to return after a year and pick up our lives once more. It was sad to say goodbye to Mum, and on reflection, the best thing we did was to go back as it was the last time, I saw her. Mum loved having the family around, and we were able to help move her from Heathfield Road to a brand-new house on Chatsworth Avenue. Mum loved her new house and it was the first time she had a new had a new kitchen which gave her a new lease of life. She enjoyed cooking once again and was soon serving up our old favourites such as meat and potato pie, apple pie and lemon meringues. I thought I was in heaven being able to taste food from my childhood. Mum got a lot of pleasure seeing us enjoying her food, and it certainly fed our souls. We stayed with Mum for the last month or so and had some happy times with her. I had hoped the children would remember her and they do, so I am thankful for that.

A few months after our return, Marg separated from her husband and returned to Fleetwood. She had given birth to a lovely little boy while we were away, and I missed them. It was however, the right decision for her at that time as she was able to spend some quality time with Mum before she passed away.

I sometimes think back to the decisions we made about our lives and the chances we have taken, but they have usually turned out to our advantage. We have also spent a lot of money travelling backwards and forwards to England, but I have no regrets, and I think the quote from Princess Diana "lead from the heart, not the head" puts my actions into perspective. I don't have any regrets, life for us has been a bit of an adventure, and we have shared lots of those adventures with our family. We have had to stick together and face the many challenges that came our way, and I think we are all the better for those experiences.

CHAPTER EIGHTEEN

My Nursing Career

"When I think about all the patients and their loved ones that I have worked with over the years I know most of them don't remember me nor I them, but I do know that I gave a little piece of myself to each of them and they to me and those threads make up the beautiful tapestry in my mind that is my career in nursing"

Donna Wilk Cardillo

I REALLY CAN'T END MY story until I have talked about my nursing career and the layers I have had to peel away while endeavouring to achieve it. I never thought about being a nurse when I was younger, not like my sister Janet who had wanted nothing more, than to be a nurse. Jan succeeded in her career through determination and hard work, and at times faced great adversary in making her dream a reality. Janet has cared for people from a young age, and it came natural to her. Throughout childhood, Mum relied on Jan, who did all that Mum asked of her in such an unselfish way. On the other hand, I did not even think about what I wanted to do when I was grown up. It wasn't until I became a nurse-aid through necessity that the seed planted in my head took many more years to sprout.

When David started school, I decided to pursue the possibility of a nursing career, after all, the children were growing up, and I believed I could cope with the demands of study and shift-work with the help of Dave; I was certainly ready for a challenge. I made an application to the nursing school in Christchurch because nursing at this stage was still hospital-based. I managed to get an interview, which I thought went well, but unfortunately, I didn't fit the entry criteria as I had no formal educational qualifications. I was, however, offered a place on the Enrolled nursing course at Burwood Hospital. Although I was disappointed I thought this would be the right path to take in my quest to be a Registered Nurse. I completed the training and enjoyed the challenges that came my way and even won the practical prize at graduation. I was offered a position working at the hospital, and that is where I started my career. Burwood Hospital, was the specialist hospital for burns at that time and I gained a lot of experience working in that speciality and saw some horrific burn injuries. I then went on to work in a cardiac ward at Princess Margaret Hospital. It was nearer home for me, and it also gave me a fantastic clinical experience. We had many cardiac arrests, and although frightening, I learned to be calm, deal with them as part of a team, and be supportive of each other. I still longed to be a Registered Nurse as there were limitations to the clinical practice of an Enrolled Nurse. Getting the O levels I needed seemed like a mammoth task to me, though, and I wasn't sure how I would manage to work and get to night school at the same time.

We returned to England in 1982; once again, we were missing our families, and to be honest, we just wanted a change. The only problem was, much to my horror, Trudy, our oldest daughter, didn't want to leave NZ. Trudy was only sixteen at the time, and I could not persuade her to change her mind. She told us she wanted her independence and had no interest in England. She had a boyfriend and was quite happy with her life in Christchurch, so we decided to go without her, which was very hard for me to do. Her best friend lived next door to us, and Trudy went to live at her house. Her mother was a nice lady who promised she would look out for Trudy, and if there were any problems, she would contact us. It was, however, a wrench for us, and we never stopped worrying about her. Trudy did eventually come to Fleetwood for a holiday but she had no intention of making it permanent.

I started to look for a job but discovered my NZ qualification was not applicable to the National Health Service in the UK. I was disappointed, but I managed to secure a role in the Intensive Care Unit at Blackpool Victoria Hospital, near where we lived. They wanted someone who would adapt to that stressful area and assist the nurses, restock, and generally help wherever you could. It was having that NZ qualification and experience, although not accepted, which made me an ideal candidate as I ticked all of those boxes. I stayed in the unit for about three years, and I loved it. It was the work on the unit which pressed me into action to gain those O levels but with a new urgency. I decided to enrol at night school and managed to get five O levels in a year, which was arduous work as I was working full time. I still keep in contact with five of the nurses who worked in the unit, and they became good friends. The Consultant working in the ICU suggested I get some theatre experience before we moved back to NZ, so I took her advice and moved to the operating theatres. I adapted well to that environment, and again made a lot of friends and had lots of fun. Although we didn't stay in England, on reflection, it was the best time of my life, and I have precious memories of the people I worked alongside. I was so grateful for the experience it gave me, and I felt well prepared to apply for Registered nurse training when we returned to New Zealand. We had nearly four years in England, but we wanted to return to NZ. We missed our life there, which was so different from our lives in the UK. Trudy and Sam were back in NZ, and I missed them. Sam had decided she wanted to return about a year earlier.

We chose not to go back to Christchurch because we were worried about job prospects for Dave. Jobs could be hard to get during the mid 1980's, so we flew to Auckland and stayed with our friends who lived in Browns Bay. They helped us to settle into the area, and we were grateful for their support. Auckland seemed such a big city after living in Christchurch, and it took us a little while to navigate the suburbs, roads, and the increased population. We decided to move to the North Shore, and I got a job at North Shore Hospital in the surgical ward. It felt a little daunting at first as I hadn't practised as an Enrolled Nurse for nearly five years, but I settled well and quickly became part of the team. I enquired about doing my Registered Nurse training again, but it had changed from being hospital-based to a tertiary setting. I now had to pay to be a nurse and we didn't have the money. I could see my ambition slowly slipping away. After a few years of working full-time, we did eventually find ourselves financially stable enough for me to start nurse training. It wasn't until 1990 that I felt confident to apply for a place at college, the family had all flown the nest, and although I had to take a student loan, financially we could manage. I had a job as Matron at a preparatory school in Remuera, and we lived on-site in a beautiful flat overlooking Rangitoto, an extinct volcanic island in the Hauraki Gulf. My job was to care for the needs of the boarders who lived at the school during the week. I shall never forget my experience at that school, and it was a privilege to look after the boys and share a little of their lives. The school permitted me to attend college during the day and be on duty as usual in the evenings and nights. I even managed to have breakfast and dinner with the boarders so I could catch up with them, and the arrangement worked well for us all. The boarding house had closed down when I started to do clinical work, so I was able to work casually at the hospital, which helped keep our finances on an even keel.

I was working on the surgical ward the day I received my final results. It was hard to concentrate on my job that morning as the ward was buzzing, and everyone was giving me the thumbs-up of encouragement. My tummy was acting like it had a whole bunch of butterflies fluttering in it. I decided to go home at lunchtime to see if the letter with my results had arrived and there it was in my mailbox sitting quite innocently, not knowing the importance of its contents. With trepidation, I opened the letter, my eyes scanning to the most crucial information, and there it was, I had passed. To say I was overjoyed is an understatement, but I was now a Registered Nurse with all the responsibility and duty expected from that profession. I went back to work to give them the excellent news expecting to finish the day as a third-year nursing student, but the Charge Nurse called me into the office to congratulate me and presented me with the epaulettes of a staff nurse. I was so proud to put them on, and she then offered me a full-time permanent position as a Staff Nurse in her ward. I floated out of her office, and one of the other staff nurses handed me the drug keys in recognition of my new status. All I could think about was that I had made it, all those years of dreaming about being a Registered Nurse had become a reality. My career progressed from there, and I went on to do my Degree the following year. I ended up working mainly in the Emergency Department of large hospitals, two of which were very busy trauma hospitals. While working in one of the larger hospitals, I did a six-month paediatric post-graduate course and became a Paediatric Nurse Specialist in the care of children who presented to the emergency department with an acute illness.

We came to Australia in 2000, and I was lucky to secure a job at Rockingham Hospital, which had an Emergency Department. It was much smaller than the ones I had worked in, which was good as I needed to master a very different health system. After about six weeks, the Charge Nurse was going on leave, and I decided to apply for the relief position as I thought it would be an opportunity to get to know the hospital and the medical system, which was quite different from that of New Zealand. They decided to split the position between myself and another nurse, so we both did three weeks each. After the challenge of being in charge of the Emergency Department, I was offered a relief After Hour Managers position, which I accepted and did for quite a few years. The job was challenging and sometimes tricky; however, I learnt many skills having to work with people who had different skill sets and who certainly had different temperaments. My last years as a nurse were happy ones, and I am so grateful for the experiences that came my way. I decided to take leave without pay and go travelling in a new caravan we had just purchased. It was the best decision we made, and six months later, I ended up giving my notice to Rockingham Hospital and I started a new professional journey that will stay with me forever. I worked as a Manager in the outback of Western Australia nursing, mainly Aboriginal people, which proved to be both challenging and daunting. The health needs of our Indigenous people are many, and it was a privilege to work with them and an experience I will never forget. I also worked as the Clinical Nurse Coordinator at one of the Regional hospitals, which I did for nearly three years. I often had to relieve the Director of Nursing, which was a massive challenge for me, not only being in charge of the hospital but also the nursing outposts of a remote Aboriginal town and a nurse post housed at a popular tourist destination. I also worked in a country town as a Clinical Nurse Manager in charge of a small hospital, which was also a big challenge. The job was only supposed to be for six weeks, but I ended up staying there for six months. My last job was as a Senior Project Officer working on a multi-million dollar Medical Imaging contract, something I had never done before but one that I enjoyed immensely.

I started my career as a mature aged student but managed to care for many people, reach great heights, make many friendships, and even exceeded beyond my own expectations. There are many stories to be told about my nursing career, but that again would be a book in itself.

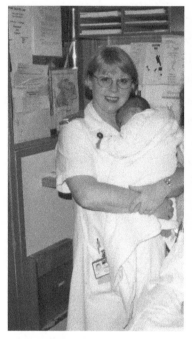

Happy days in the Kimberley

**Jennifer in the Emergency
Department in Middlemore
Hospital NZ**

THE END

I WILL LEAVE THE STORY of my early years here and hope you have enjoyed reading about my young life, my family, and my Mum and Dad. My journey has been a little like a fairground ride with its ups and downs, but I've always been ready to hop on again and give it another try.

My family has slowly got smaller and I never expected to lose my siblings at such a young age, a sadness which will always stay with me. It has been a reflective journey though, remembering memories that were both happy and sad while growing up. I am thankful to have experienced all of those challenges in my life, good and bad, as they have shaped me into who I am today. Additionally, I have put into perspective a few of my regrets, facing them with integrity and introspection and accepting responsibility for them. By gently peeling those layers away, which at times has felt raw and awkward, I can see me as I was and who I have now become. I have seen life, there is no doubt about that, and this self-exposure has given me an understanding of how my family and ancestors have played their part. I can even see some of my ancestors' traits of determination and resilience dotted throughout my years. My ancestors have helped me to see life as it really is, there is nothing promised, it continues from generation to generation, we live, we die, and the bit inbetween is what really matters.

They have given me a love for family, which sits deeply in my heart. I now know I am a better person, and writing my story has been the catalyst in discovering that fact.

PART TWO

Stories of my ancestors and
their link to Fleetwood

"I am bound to them, though I cannot look into their eyes or hear their voices. I honour their history, and I cherish their lives. I will tell their story; I will remember them"

Author Unknown

THE PURSUIT OF FAMILY HISTORY and origins tends to be shaped by several motives, including the desire to carve out a place for one's family in a broader historical picture. It gives you a sense of responsibility to preserve the past for future generations, and self-satisfaction in authentic storytelling. (Wikipedia)

How true this statement is for me and each of those elements underpins my motives. There is no doubt genealogy is a complex process using historical records to establish kinship, and I have not been so lucky in this respect. The only legal documents I have are records I have had to purchase with only a few photos coming from the family. Maybe most of the information has been lost, or perhaps it is sitting in someone's cupboard, or perhaps the family doesn't realize what is essential to a person doing the research. I do urge everyone who reads my book and has an interest in family history to start thinking about how to gather their information. It would help if you began gathering your documents for the future, materials that could bring your ancestors to life for you, or for someone else to tell their story.

I have so loved researching my family tree and never expected that I would succeed and uncover so many facts about those who came before me. When I first started to look at the lives of my ancestors, I realized their lives mirrored my own family in so many ways, which was almost uncanny. I had a great grandfather and his wife, who drowned in a dock at Bristol. There was an uncle who drowned at sea after falling overboard from a ship and a great uncle who drowned while fishing at sea. Families that lost loved ones at a young age and families that were poor. There were young women having children out of wedlock which was not sociably accepted in those days. I still have so much more to discover, but there is no doubt that my family ploughed the land, sailed the seas, and experienced loss on a large scale.

I wanted to share these stories of hardship, tragedy, and love, but the further back I went, the harder it was to capture their lives with any certainty, but I do feel privileged to have explored the lives of just a few, which I will share with you. It has been a challenge to document my family tree as there are hundreds of people in the tree going back in time to the mid-1600s. There are still so many more stories to be told, and more facts to uncover. I acknowledge this work will not get finished in my lifetime, a challenge for someone in the future to carry on. The following stories will hopefully bring to life these long-forgotten but still loved families. They are all researched with care, and it is with unconditional love and respect that I divulge their stories; they perhaps may not have wanted me to tell. But they are important stories to be told and with an acknowledgement that they all "had to do what they had to do" to be able to survive.

JIM GORST
29/06/1889-17/11/1947 (my grandfather)
married Mary Rimmer

JIM GORST (DAD'S FATHER) WAS born on June 29th, 1889, at 4 Bridge Road, Poulton, Lancaster. At the time of his birth, his father was a coal dealer. His father was James Gorst and his mother, Nancy Gorst, nee Armer. He married Mary Rimmer on 29/06/1910 at St Peter's Church in Fleetwood, and they both lived at 13 Gordon Road, Fleetwood. At the time of their marriage, he was twenty-one, and a Carter by trade. A letter in his war record states he was a "thoroughly experience horseman," and as a Carter, in those days, he would have been a driver of a horse-drawn carrier. They used these sorts of light wheeled carriers for transporting goods to Fleetwood pier, which opened in 1910, and it would have provided work for many in the town. The pier had a promenade deck with an ornate oriental-style pavilion added the following year, and the jetty was 600ft long. It would have been a large project, and I often wonder if grandad had a hand in carting building materials to the site. He could have been involved in many construction projects in Fleetwood at that time. He worked for the council as a horseman in the early days then as a gardener in the Municipal Parks department for many years. I look at the lovely photos of the flowers in full bloom in the Marine Gardens during 1930 and 1940 and, I think of him. He was involved with the planting and upkeep of those gardens, and you can see by the old photographs, the men put a lot of pride into their work.

He joined the Army on 02/08/1915 as a Gunner, at age twenty-five, and he was married with three children. They lived at 2 Church Street, Fleetwood. It must have been hard for his wife Mary, left alone with their three children, age four, three, and six months old. He enlisted into the Royal Field Artillery and was attached to the Howitzer Brigade. The RFA was the most significant arm of the artillery and provided support for the British Army. He was responsible for the medium calibre guns, and howitzers used close to the front line in France. He was also deployed with the Expeditionary Force to the Mediterranean in 1916 and later the Expeditionary Force to France. In 1916 he was hospitalized, and I expect injured in France, but apart from the documentation stating he was in a

Torquay hospital in 1916, I am unable to find the cause of his admission. It must have been tough for him to leave his family and for whatever reason, and there could be many, a report in 1916 stated he was absent without leave. He was discharged from the Army in 1920 and awarded the Victory Medal and the British War Medal.

His wife Mary died in 1928, age forty; they were living at 10 Victoria Street then, and it must have been difficult for him as my dad was only seven at that time. After her death, they moved to 9 Albert Street in Fleetwood. I think grandad must have gone through a few turbulent years after her death as there are many pieces of his jigsaw, which I can't explain. His son William Henry who would have been fifteen when his mother died, didn't stay with the family. He went to lodge at the house of a Mrs Stony in Victoria Street and I think he may have been going to sea at that stage, but I'm not sure. He still lived there when he got lost overboard in 1936, and an account in the newspaper said his landlady was aware of his death. I found it unusual that he never stayed with his father, and wonder why. Grandad also had a conviction for breaking into a warehouse and theft in 1930, two years after his wife died. The courts wrote to the war office for verification of his war record, which stated his "character had been assessed as very good," so I think that may have saved him from going to prison. Another mystery surrounds a newspaper clipping about a Mrs Elizabeth Gorst stabbing a woman in the pub, and her address was given as 9 Albert Street. Grandad never remarried, so it is, and will remain a mystery as to her identity.

Grandad eventually moved with my Dad to his daughter Margaret's house at 11 Oxford Road and died there on November 17th, 1947, a year before I was born. He was only fifty-eight and died from cardiac failure, chronic myocarditis, and bronchitis. Dr. Kerr signed his death certificate. He was buried with his mother and father in Fleetwood Cemetery and

Grandad in his army uniform

not with his wife and daughter, which I thought was odd. His grave is in the non-conformist area of Fleetwood cemetery, so it may have been something to do with his beliefs. I did note a discrepancy in his burial records, which states the date of burial is March 2nd, but in another document, it said November 21st, which is, in fact, the correct date. His burial record number is 5431, and I did try to find his grave but was unsuccessful.

MARY RIMMER
22/09/1887-10/08/1928 (my grandmother) *married Jim Gorst*

MARY RIMMER (DAD'S MOTHER) WAS born on September 22nd, 1887, at 36 Cop Lane Fleetwood. Her father was William Rimmer, a farmworker, and her mother was Jane Rimmer nee Gradwell. Mary was a servant for the Atkinson Family at Nook Farm in 1901 when she was only thirteen. She married Jim Gorst on 29/06/1910 at St Peter's Church in Fleetwood, and they both lived at 13 Gordon Road, Fleetwood. At the time of their marriage, Mary was twenty-two, and her father was deceased. Their first child Margaret was born in 1911, and Jim, Margaret's father, was now working as a railway labourer.

In 1915 when Jim joined the Army, they had three children. The youngest Earl Kenneth was only a few months old. It must have been difficult in all aspects of Mary's life as not only would food rationing be in place but also a loss of their income would have impacted enormously. Many families found themselves in positions where they lost a proportion or, in some cases, all of their household income. The man, however, could claim a Separation Allowance, which consisted of a portion of a soldier's pay, which was generally matched by the Government to ensure that the soldier's dependents were not left destitute. It must have been very sad when Mary lost her baby Kathleen in 1920, a year before my Dad was born. Kathleen was only one month old and died of convulsions, something that just wouldn't happen today, as it was probably due to a high temperature. Mary died in Fleetwood Hospital when she was forty of endocarditis, heart failure, and miscarriage, her husband Jim was by her side. They had been married eighteen years, and I should think that

Jim would have been devastated. My Dad's older sisters Margaret and Beatrice, looked after my Dad, and I know they remained close throughout the years. I can remember Dad always visited them when he was in from sea. Visiting them on Christmas Day was part of our ritual regardless of the cold weather, and it would have been important to Dad to have their influence on us as children. Fleetwood Cemetery is Mary's resting place alongside Kathleen, her baby daughter. I felt sad that I couldn't find any records relating to the location of her burial, as I would have liked to have visited her grave.

Mary my grandmother

MARGARET ANN GORST
1911-1999 (Dad's eldest sister) *married Matthew Woods*

Margaret Ann Woods nee Gorst born on January 30th, 1911, and was the eldest child of Jim and Mary Gorst. They lived at 13 Gordon Road when she was born. Her birth certificate records her father as being a railway labourer at that time. Aunty Marg married Henry Samuel Varty in Birkenhead, Cheshire, in 1931 when she was twenty, and they had a daughter Sheila. I think Aunty Marg was a housekeeper in Birkenhead. Henry Varty died young, and Aunty Marg remarried on October 21st, 1936, at St Peters Church in Fleetwood. Her second husband, Matthew Woods, was twenty-four and a fisherman, he lived at 49 Mowbray Road. His father was also named Matthew, which was usual in those days. I found researching our family history was made much easier by the sons having their father's Christian name. Sadly, Matthew died of tuberculosis when he was twenty-nine after only five years of marriage, leaving four children. Their marriage certificate shows she lived at 9 Albert Street, Fleetwood, and we know that was where her father and siblings lived. The document also indicates she did housework as a job. We also know 1936 the year of her wedding, was when her brother, William Henry, was lost at sea, another sad event in their lives. My cousin Jimmy told me that when his granddad Jim went to live with them in Oxford Road, Aunty Marg use to go mad at him because he always smelt of horses. He also told me they use to have chickens in their back garden. Aunty Marg died on March 23rd, 1999, aged eighty-eight and was found dead on the settee by her son Jimmy. He always went to her house every morning to light the fire and it would have been a shock for him as Aunty Marg must have passed away the night before. She died of Ischaemic Heart Disease, and I think she would probably have had a heart attack.

WILLIAM HENRY GORST
1913-1936 (Dad's brother)

William was the eldest son of Jim and Mary Gorst, and he was lost overboard from the trawler *Orilla* on January 31st, 1936, when he was just twenty-three. The *Orilla* was a Fleetwood trawler sailing out of Hull, and he had only been there for five weeks. He had been lodging in Victoria Street for eight years before moving to Hull, and his landlady was a Mrs E Stoney. His mum and dad lived in Victoria Street at the time of his mother's death, and it appears that William Henry went to lodge at the Stoney household which was in the same street. He was only fifteen at the time and I do wonder why he didn't stay with his dad when his mother died. Tragically, my brother Harry christened William Henry, also drowned. I included a transcription about his death in 1936 which I found in the fiche files of the Fleetwood Chronicle at the library.

LOST AT SEA

Throwing Out the Log/Tragedy on Second Voyage

He was lost overboard on his second voyage in a Fleetwood trawler sailing out of Hull. This was the tragic fate of William Henry Gorst, a 23-year-old deckhand of Fleetwood. Mr. Gorst was in the trawler "Orilla" bound for the White Sea fishing grounds, and news of the tragedy reached Fleetwood on

Wednesday. Details are not yet fully known, Mr. Gorst was drowned on January 31ˢᵗ but as the trawler is still at sea the only information received by his father Mr. Jim Gorst who lives at 9 Albert Street Fleetwood is a copy of a letter from the skipper G Booth of the Orilla giving brief details.

The letter states that on January 31ˢᵗ, Mr. Gorst was lost overboard. At 2 pm, he had been ordered to *throw out the log, and while executing this duty, he slipped and fell into the sea. The alarm was given by the third hand who was quite close but not near enough to render assistance. The Chief engineer also witnessed the incident. The boat was stopped immediately and then brought alongside the man, but before he could be caught hold of, he sank and was not seen again.

Mr. William Henry Gorst was a native of Fleetwood and, for eight years until five weeks ago, had lived in lodgings in Victoria Street. He had been going to sea since he was 17 years of age, and five weeks ago, he went to Hull, where he signed on in the Marr and Son LTD of Fleetwood but sailing out of Hull, the east coast port. He made a trip to Bear Island and was on his second voyage out of Hull and apparently on his first or second day out of port when he met with his death. His Fleetwood landlady Mrs. H.E. Stoney received a telegraph last night from one of the drowned man's friends saying he had lost his life. He was the eldest son of Mr. Jim Gorst, and his two brothers and two sisters live in Fleetwood.

* The log was an instrument that was thrown over the stern of the ship to measure the speed and distance of the ship, which was done every 24 hours in those days.

Fleetwood Chronicle Fiche film available at Fleetwood library

EARL KENNETH
1915-1980 (Dad's brother) married to Edith Bevan in 1938 and then remarried in 1960 to Norah Ellis.

I don't know too much about him even though he lived in Fleetwood. I believe he went to sea for a time and he was also in the Navy. I think Uncle Ken may have been a bit of a lad in his younger days as I accidentally found an account of this misdemeanour from the Fleetwood Chronicle while I was searching the fiche files in Fleetwood library. The police caught him breaking into Fleetwood baths.

"SHOUTED SCATTER"

Three Fleetwood Young Men on Breaking-in Charge

Three Fleetwood young men, XXXXXX (21) of Kent Street, and Earl Kenneth Gorst (22) of Park Avenue, both deckhands, and XXXXXX (18), a factory hand were committed to Preston Sessions by Fleetwood magistrates today, on a charge of breaking and entering the Fleetwood Baths Café, and stealing cigarettes and sweets to the value of £1 5s2d. Acting-Supt Craven said P.C. Newstead was on duty on the Fleetwood Promenade shortly after 1 am on Tuesday when he heard a noise of breaking wood. He saw the three accused climbing over the wall of the baths, They told the constable they had been swimming, but when he questioned them as to their bulging pockets, xxxxxx shouted "scatter" An application for bail was allowed in each case, in personal sureties of £10 and a further surety of £10.

The newspaper account made me laugh as I could just see these three young men trying to scatter in every direction.

BEATRICE GORST
1917-2010 (Dad's sister) Married William Crowford

Beatrice married William Crowford in 1937 and lived for most of her married life at 4 Seabank Road, a house I remember well. The house is near the promenade, so it was a good stopover when we went to the beach, which we did often. Uncle Bill was a fisherman and a kind man; he had survived a trawler tragedy himself on New Years' Eve 1954. The trawler *Evelyn Rose* struck the shore at about 1 am due to her passing the wrong side of a navigation light. The trawler hit the rocks, and she slipped into deep water and sank within minutes about 100 yards from the shore. Twelve crewmen drowned and two were saved, one was Uncle Bill. Another sad event for our town and may they all RIP.

William (Bill) died in February 1985; they had been married for forty-eight years and had six children together. Aunty Beat lost two of her children, Kenneth born and died in 1942 and her lovely daughter Margaret Vera who passed away in 1987, aged forty-eight, who I remember with love. In later years Beatrice moved to Styan Street, where she lived until her death. Aunty Beat was a wonderful Auntie who never forgot us, and I was so lucky to have many visits with her when home from Australia. Auntie Beat managed to give me information about the family, which made such a difference in clarifying the information I was collecting. Aunty Beat died in 2016, age ninety-nine, a sad loss for the family and a true matriarch. The family gathered together the following year to celebrate her 100th birthday. Remembering her in this way is a testimony to the love her family had for her.

JAMES GORST
1855-1929 *(my great grandfather) Married Nancy Armer*

James was born on April 3rd, 1855; his father was Henry, and his mother was Ann (Townley). He was born in Poulton Le Sands, Lancaster, and his father was a lighthouse man. Poulton Le Sands was a small fishing village on the shores of Morecombe Bay and, along with two other communities Torresholme and Bare, became Morecombe, named as a fashionable seaside town in those days. The Gazette wrote about Poulton Le Sands in 1829 to say "We have little doubt that Poulton will soon become the first fashionable resort in the neighbourhood, and we can't be astonished if it does, considering how easily it is accessible, and the beautiful and picturesque view presented from its coast." (The Rise of Morecombe 1820-1862 R.G. Armstrong B.A.) James and his family lived in Morecombe during that crucial period The development of Morecombe and the formation of the railway and harbour company would have given many men employment at that time. The railways brought thousands of visitors from Yorkshire to Morecombe apart from 1854 when there was an outbreak of Cholera. James married Nancy Armer in 1878 when he was a farm labourer, a few of the census information shows he was an agricultural worker for many years. The 1881 census taken three years after he was married records a stepson Thomas Corless who was aged three. Nancy could have been at the end of her pregnancy when they married, or Thomas was a newborn. Either way, James was not his father. In the 1891 census, it is documented Thomas as their son, and his surname was now Armer, his mother's name before her marriage. The 1911 census shows Thomas Gorst age twelve being their grandson, and I am guessing this is Thomas Corless's son. I am only documenting this as it was a story that needed unravelling and someone may want to delve further into the surname Corless. James and Nancy had nine children together, but sadly, apart from Jim, they all died young, and it was deplorable that in 1907 they lost two daughters, Margaret Ann, twenty-six, and Susannah, twenty-three in the same year. It must have been a sad road they travelled to lose all of their children; Jim, my grandad, is the only one that survived adulthood. I wonder why James and Nancy chose to be buried in the non-conformist area of the cemetery. They baptized all of their children so they must have been believers. Maybe they had lost their faith with the death of all their children, but I guess we will never know. James died in Fleetwood Hospital on February 25th, 1929, aged seventy-four, he lived at 10 Victoria Street at the time of his death, and his son Jim was with him. His death certificate states he was formally a horse driver, and Dr Wylie signed the death certificate. He died of cellulitis of the elbow, toxaemia and heart failure.

NANCY GORST NEE ARMER
1859-1917 (my great grandmother) *Married James Gorst*

Nancy was born at Jogger Hill Cockerham on the February 26th, 1859. Her father was Thomas Armer and her mother, Margaret Armer, nee Preston. Margaret was illiterate as Nancy's birth certificate shows her mark as a signature, which was not uncommon. Her father Thomas was an agricultural worker, again that was also usual for those days as the land was the primary source of income for many. One in every six males over the age of ten was a farm labourer in 1851, a sign that farming was highly significant. In 1861 Nancy had seven siblings, and her mother Margaret died of Phthisis (Tuberculosis) in1866, aged thirty-eight when Nancy was only seven years old. Her father went on to marry again and had a further six children, so he had fourteen children in all. They all lived in a small dwelling called Jogger Hill, which must have been overcrowded, and I should imagine their conditions would have been awful compared to today's standards. I have been to where this little house was situated, and it looks quite different now, but it was such a privilege to see it. There is a lot of information regarding the Armer's and this could be a work of art on its own, and something I would like to do in the future.

The 1871 census shows that Nancy was a servant at the Manor Inn in Cockerham when she was only twelve; the population of Cockerham at that time was 803, according to the census. The Manor Inn, as it is today, was previously named the Plough, and the old Manor Inn is now a private residence. Nancy married James Gorst in 1878 when she was nineteen, and as we already know, had a son called Thomas, who James adopted. I am unsure if this adoption was official. We know Nancy went on to have nine children, and most of their children died as infants apart from Margaret Ann and Susannah, who both died in the same year 1907. Margaret Ann was twenty-six and died in childbirth from pre-eclampsia, and Susannah was twenty-three and died of T.B. I can't imagine how that felt to lose her two daughters in the same year, and I do sometimes wonder how life can be so cruel. I think Nancy must have had a sad time with the deaths of her children and wonder how she was able to overcome those brutal events. She was living at a time when disease and poverty were shared, and it impacted her family greatly. I hope Nancy had some happy times with James, my great-grandfather, they had been married 39 years when she died. Nancy died on August 24th, 1917, when she was fifty-eight. Her death certificate shows the cause of death to be 1. Dilation of the heart and 2. Dropsy (An old term for the swelling of soft tissues due to the accumulation of excess water), and Dr Preston signed the death certificate. Her daughter-in-law, Mary (my grandmother), was present at her death, so they must have lived with their son Jim and Mary at 10 Victoria Street where my father was born. Jim did not remarry and went on to live a further twelve years. They are buried together with their son Jim in Fleetwood cemetery.

I always wondered why my Dad was christened Jim and not James as one would expect, and I was to discover that one of James and Nancy children was christened James in 1882 but died. A few years later, they had another boy and named him Jim, which would have honoured their previous son without taking his name away from him. It appears to be important in those days to name any male children after their father, usually the firstborn son. It was also not an unusual practice to use the same names again if they had lost a child. When I am in the UK, I always visit Cockerham, where Nancy was born. St Michaels Church, in particular, is special to me as this is where many of my ancestors lay and it is where I feel the most connected to my ancestors. When I first walked the path up to the church, I could imagine people who lived long ago, walking arm in arm to church on a Sunday, dressed in their best clothes and looking happy. I could also imagine horses and carts trotting up the hill, carrying families to worship. I also saw another picture of snow piled high, people huddled together climbing towards the church, their misty breaths dispersing into the air. There is no other place in my life that I get those images of lives that came before me, and they are precious. Mary Armstrong nee Gorst's grave is near the front entrance to the church, and I left flowers last time I was there. I was lucky enough to talk with David Armer, a distant relative, who lives in the village and he gave me information regarding the family which I was very grateful for. I was also thrilled to see a photograph of Nancy's brother John who was born in 1853 hanging in their hallway. He was a very jolly-looking man who was a farm labourer, and it was fascinating to put a face to one of my ancestors.

HENRY GORST
1831-1902 (my great-great-grandfather)
Married Ann Townley

Henry was born in 1831 at Winmarleigh, Garstang, Lancashire. His mother, Mary Gorst/Goose, was around sixteen years old and unmarried at that time. I have been unable to find who his father was, there is a blank space on his birth and marriage certificates and I wonder if he knew himself. His mother went on to marry John Armstrong, and they had ten children together, so he became part of a large family. His step-father and mother lived at Bank End in Cockerham for many years, and this is where he would have lived. He married Ann Townley in 1850 when he was nineteen, and they had eight children together. Henry worked mainly as a farmer and agricultural worker and when Henry was fifty, he was a Carter Van Man. He was still working when he was seventy as a market gardener. Henry died in Lancaster, age seventy-one, and his wife died ten years later.

ANN TOWNLEY
1831-1913 (my great-great-grandmother)
Married Henry Gorst

Ann Townley was born in 1831 at Morecombe, and her parents were James Townley and Mary Mayor. I believe Ann may have been a member of the Townley family who were landowners around the Clitheroe area but it is a story that needs further research. Mary had one brother and three sisters, Henry and Ann, had eight children together. Ann died of old age in Carnforth when she was eighty-one years old.

MARY ARMSTRONG
nee GOOSE/GORST1815-1884 (my great-great-great grandmother) *Married John Armstrong*

Mary was born in 1815 at Slaidburn, Yorkshire, and I presume her family moved there from Lancashire. There was a name change during those years from Goose to Gorst, and I don't know the real reason, but names from the 15th century came from a variety of sources, including places, nicknames, estate names, occupations, and physical attributes. Maybe the family kept geese on the land, who knows, but one thing I do know is I am glad it was changed; it was bad enough to be called ghosty, and spooky at School, let alone be called goosy goosy gander, or she's a goose. Her father was William Goose/Gorst, and her mother was Ann Harrison, she had one sister named Ellen Goose. William, her father, was a landowner, and when he died, he left everything to his wife and sons. He did leave Mary and her son Henry a small amount of money which interestingly was less than her brothers received but was probably usual for those times.

Mary's married a farmer called John Armstrong and they lived all their married life in Cockerham. Mary died in 1884 and was buried alongside her husband John in St Michael Church, Cockerham, they had ten children together. I feel an affinity with Mary, my great-great-great-grandmother, as she was the first ancestor I discovered and the first grave I visited. I would like to know more about her, another project!

WILLIAM RIMMER
1858- 1892 (My great grandfather) *Married Jane Gradwell*

William Rimmer was born in 1858 at Lytham, Lancashire, the fifth child of Jeffrey Rimmer and Mary Mansergh. His father was a Master Mariner and sailed mostly out of Preston in Lancashire. William is my grandmother, Mary's father, so my great grandfather, and he too, had witnessed many tragedies in his life. He lost his mother and father on the same day when he was twelve, they both drowned in Bristol Harbour in 1869, leaving their six children orphaned. It must have been devastating for the family as they were left destitute. Voluntary subscriptions and the church were the only support they had. Their nearest relatives were William Mansergh, their mothers' brother, and Thomas Rimmer, their fathers' brother, neither of whom were able to look after them. William Mansergh was a tailer in Clifton Street in Lytham and, according to the orphanage documentation, "Has been an industrious, hardworking man" and he himself had a large family, so could not look after them. The other Uncle, Thomas Rimmer was a grocer in Preston, and the documentation states "Has not been very fortunate in business," and they believed they couldn't look to him for help. They also felt the two eldest children were able to fend for themselves being 19 and 13. It was the youngest three children they were concerned about as the 13-year-old girl was already in service. I think the eldest girl was in America and 'm not sure of her timeline, which is something I need to do. They tried to keep William and Samuel the two youngest brothers together but were unsuccessful. Samuel ended up in the Muller Orphans Home at Ashley Downs in Bristol, leaving behind Jeffrey and William. The elder boys went to the Swinton Industrial School, which was for pauper children in Manchester. William and Jeffrey, his older brother, were in the Swinton School for two years, and interestingly, William left a few months before Jeffrey, and I'm not sure why or where they went to. Unfortunately, and sadly, I have real doubts the family ever met up with one another again.

In the 1881 census, William, twenty-two, was a servant (ploughman) at Mythop Lodge in Weeton with Preece, a village not too far from Fleetwood. He married in 1887 when he was twenty-seven and his wife Jane Gradwell lived at 36 Cop Lane Fleetwood, the marriage certificate states he was a Farm Labourer. They had four children together, but in June 1892, they lost their son Jeffrey at seven months old to bronchial - pneumonia, and in the December William, himself died of pneumonia aged thirty. They lived at 8 Cop Lane, and Jane was about two months pregnant at the time of Williams's death. It must have been terrible for Jane to lose her husband and child, but fate didn't leave it there, Jane went on to have her baby boy in July and named him William after his father, but he also died when he was two months old. His death certificate shows he died from Marasmus, and according to Wikipedia, this is a form of severe malnutrition. Marasmus is an energy deficiency that reduces the bodyweight to less than 62% of the healthy body weight of a child.

I do wonder what happened to Jane after William died, having three children to feed and clothe, my grandmother Mary was only four, and Ellen, her sister, was two years old. Did Jane have post-natal depression, or was she so financially needy that she couldn't feed herself properly, therefore, produced less breast milk for her baby. It is indeed a sad story of William's short life, losing both his parents in a tragic accident, being put into an orphanage, and then losing two of his children. William and Jane were only married for five years before he died, and I do hope they were happy years, but I have a feeling they were anything but.

JANE GRADWELL
1858 (My great grandmother) *Married William Rimmer*

Jane was born in1869, and although her marriage certificates state her father was John Gradwell, he was actually her grandfather as John's eldest daughter Eleanor had Jane when she was twenty-one. It seems evident that Jane thought of John as her father, his name was on her marriage certificate, and it may be that John adopted her, but I cannot find any proof of this. The Gradwell's were a big Fleetwood family. They lived in a now demolished street called Cop Lane. In 1881 Jane worked as a general servant for a butcher in Lower Dock Street when she was only twelve, so I surmise her life was hard and had been hard from a young age. Jane married William on August 20th, 1887, when she was twenty. Because William was a farm labourer, they could have met through the butcher she worked for, who knows. They were married at St Peter's Church in Fleetwood, and John and Sarah Gradwell were the witnesses. Jane was left a widow at only twenty-five and remarried four years later in 1896 to William Rudd, who was a widower. He was a chemical worker from Ireland, and they married in the Catholic church of St Mary's in Fleetwood. Unfortunately for Jane, William died in 1902, so she only had six years with him. Jane married again in 1903, her new husband John Leonard Greenwood was from London. This is where my research has stalled in regards to Jane. I hope she found some lasting happiness with John, and they lived long lives, she certainly deserved to.

GEOFFREY RIMMER
1882-1869 (my great-great-grandfather)
married Mary Mansergh

Geoffrey was born in 1822 at Hesketh Bank, his father was James Rimmer, and his mother was Alice Waring. Geoffrey was a master mariner who sailed from Preston on various coastal and foreign sailing ships. He married Mary Mansergh on December 19th, 1845, at St Cuthbert Church in Lytham. They had eight children together and lived in Clifton Street, Lytham. I should imagine it must have been a lonely life for Mary as Geoffrey would have been away for long periods at sea, but hopefully, the children would have had a stable upbringing as they lived in Lytham for many years.

In 1869 tragedy struck the family as both Geoffrey and Mary drowned in the Floating Dock at Bristol. Mary must have either been visiting her husband or had been on a journey with him. It is surmised Mary lost her footing on the gangplank and fell into the dock, and Geoffrey dived in to save her. Although Geoffrey and Mary had six children sadly, their eldest son James was drowned in a heavy sea the year before their own deaths. He was fishing at Kingston when the weather turned bad, and he was lost overboard and written in one of the letters of supporting information sent to the orphanage it states that James was a "Fine promising young man."

The other five children were left orphans, and their ages were 20, 14, 13, 11, and 7. What a sad demise for this family and I wonder why the children were not taken in by family, but as I have shown in Williams, my great grandfather's story, there was no one to call upon. Their Uncle, the tailer who lived in Lytham, was the main person assisting in finding foster homes for the children because he couldn't take them in himself. It must have been a sad and challenging decision for him to split up the family, and I'm sure it wouldn't happen today, but it shows how life was very different for people living in the 1800s. The children were at the mercy of the church and legal representatives; both appeared genuine and concerned for the children. In one of the letters I have, it shows they tried their hardest to get the two youngest, William and Samuel into somewhere together, but it didn't happen, and they were separated. I have transcribed a newspaper article relating to the drowning tragedy.

A CAPTAIN AND HIS WIFE DROWNED AT BRISTOL

A most profound sensation was created on Wednesday morning in the neighbourhood of the Sea Banks and amongst those more immediately connected with the shipping of our port, by the discovery of the bodies of Captain Geoffrey Rimmer, of the "Mary Nixon," a three-masted Schooner, which arrived in Bristol on Saturday from Leghorn and Genoa, and which is lying at "Taylor's Wharf, on the Sea Banks, and Mary, his wife, in the Floating Harbour, under circumstances which could leave no doubt that they had been drowned whilst going onboard their vessel. It appears that Captain Rimmer and his wife left the George Inn on the Butts, where they had been having some refreshment, about half-past ten o'clock on Tuesday night, both perfectly sober, and they were not seen alive afterwards. On Wednesday morning the corpse of Mrs Rimmer was seen floating on the surface of the water some distance above the "Mary Nixon" having been drifted by an under-current, and on search being made for that of her husband it was found between the vessel and the quay wall. The ship was lying about ten feet from the wharf, and the only means of communication with her was a plank some eleven of twelve inches wide. It is supposed-but is mere conjecture-that the ill-fated pair were walking along the plank when one of them-probably Mrs Rimmer fell in, and the other, in trying to render assistance, also became immersed, and both were drowned. The mate of the "Mary Nixon" went below at nine o'clock and fell asleep, and the Custom-house officer boarded on the vessel was relieved at nine o'clock, and his place was not supplied until three o'clock the next morning; so there was no one at hand to help them. Capt Rimmer was a native of Lytham,

*Lancashire and leaves a family of six children. In the course
of Wednesday afternoon Mr H.S. Wasbrough held an inquest
at St Peter's Hospital, on the bodies of the unfortunate couple.
The coroner having briefly stated the facts of the case as far as
they had come to his knowledge, and the jury having viewed the
corpses, which were those of middle-aged persons, the following
evidence was taken:*

*William Johns- I am mate of the "Mary Nixon" now lying at
Bristol. Captain Rimmer left the vessel between one and two
o'clock on Tuesday Afternoon, and his wife left shortly after
three o'clock, he having arranged to meet her at the office. I
did not hear or see of them afterwards. I went on deck till nine
o'clock at night and I then went below and fell asleep. I remained
asleep until 12 o'clock when I woke up, put out the lights, and
went to bed. The custom-house officer left about nine o'clock,
and I did not see any other officer come on board to relieve him.
When I turned out at seven o'clock on Wednesday morning, I
found there was an officer on board. Henry Cole, a waterman-
About eight o'clock on Wednesday morning I was called by
another waterman named Wolfe, to assist him in securing the
body of a female which was floating on the surface of the water.
A quantity of air had got inside the cloak the woman wore and
buoyed her up. She was about 200 yards from the vessel.*

*P.S. Job (12) I searched the corpse of Mrs Rimmer and found
2 0s 8d in gold, silver and copper monies, three foreign coins,
and some other articles. There was no mark of violence on her.*

*P.C. Barry (279) I searched the body of Captain Rimmer, and
found 7s 101/2d in silver and copper moneys, a foreign coin,
some letters, and a pocket-book containing a variety of papers.
There was no mark of violence on him.*

*After some observations from the coroner, a verdict of "Found
dead" was returned.*

West Somerset Free Press January 23rd, 1869

Their children were

James Rimmer 1846-1868 Who drowned from a fishing boat in Kingston, Bristol.

Catherine Rimmer 1849-1914 Catherine went to America and interestingly married William Crossley in November 1869 some 10 months after her parents drowning. She could have been in America when the tragedy unfolded which would have accounted for the fact that she couldn't take care of her siblings. Catherine settled in Fall River, Boston, Massachusetts, USA and went on to have four children she died on October 10th, 1914, of diabetes mellitus and is buried in Oak Grove Cemetery Plot # OG786.

Mary Alice Rimmer 1851-1855 Mary died aged four and buried in St Cuthbert's Church on December 3rd, 1855.

Elizabeth Ellen 1855 Elizabeth went into service, and although I know little about her life, I would like to find out more.

Jeffrey Rimmer 1856

William 1858

Jeffrey and William were both admitted to the Swinton Industrial School set up by the Manchester Poor Law Union on the April 17th, 1869 and they stayed there till 1871. It is interesting to note that Jeffrey and William were both admitted to Swinton on April 17th, 1869, but William was discharged a month earlier than Jeffrey on September 28th, 1871. I can only surmise that they were able to secure a place for William as a farm servant at Mythorp Lodge in Singleton, Lancashire. Jeffrey emigrated to the USA and joined his sister in 1872, he married Sophia Tetlow on Christmas Eve in 1881, and they had four children. Quite sentimentally, he named his children Jeffrey, William, James, and Alice, so I think he never forgot his family and roots. Jeffrey and

Sophia sailed back to the U.K. in 1910, but of course, William had died, and I doubt they caught up with Elizabeth and Samuel. Jeffrey was a blacksmith for all of his working life and lived in Massachusetts until he died in 1920. Samuel Rimmer was born on December 15th, 1861, at Lytham. He was eight years old when his parents drowned. Now an orphan, and they had to find a place for him to live. It was sad that he was eventually split from his family and was admitted into New Orphan House at Ashley Down in Bristol on January 19th, 1970, Orphan No 2894. The story of Reverend George Muller, who was responsible for the building of the orphanage, is an interesting one, though. Criteria for any child's admission was that they were born into a lawful marriage, had lost both parents and were in destitute circumstances. The care in this orphanage was exemplary for those times. The orphanage had a religious base and they taught the Christian belief. I'm sure Samuel would have been happy there, and although he did not have his brothers near him, he would have had stability and care. Samuel left the orphanage in 1876 after living there for six years. He went to Joseph Tyne, an engineering company as an apprentice Fitter and Turner at Barton Hill in Dorsetshire. His discharge shows he was "a believer."

MARY MANSERGH
1819-1869 (my great-great-grandmother)
Married Geoffrey Rimmer

Mary was born in 1819 at Preston, Lancashire, and she baptised at St John's Church on March 23rd, 1819. Her father was William Mansergh and her mother, Mary Barlow. Mary's daughter Elizabeth Ann was born out of wedlock in 1841 at Little Bolton. Although I have found no information about Elizabeth Ann, I have presumed she died because Mary called one of her later children Elizabeth Ellen in 1855, which is something families often did in those days.

ELIZABETH (LIZZIE) PORTER
1843-1907 (my great maternal grandmother)
Married Thomas Rogers

Lizzie was born in 1843 and baptized on October 29th at St Peters Church in Fleetwood. Lizzie was born out of wedlock to Nanny Porter, and her life was indeed full of tragedy. Lizzie lost three husbands in a short time frame, and she mainly brought up her children on her own. I cannot comprehend the hardships she would have experienced, no NHS, no benefits, living in a small cramped house, but always trying to do her best. The children were all baptised, and they loved her. My grandfather had a tattoo memorial on his arm, which was a gravestone, and it said, "In memory of my mother." I am going to mention her husbands before she married my great grandfather so that I can give you an understanding of how her journey progressed and the heartache she would have experienced.

Lizzie married Hugh Harrison, a fisherman/sailmaker in 1864 when she was twenty-one, and they had two children, Ellen born 1865 and James, born in 1866. Her husband Hugh drowned in the River Wyre on November 20th, 1866, when he was only twenty-six leaving Lizzie a widow at twenty-three with a small child, and a newborn baby. Lizzie then married William Tilley in 1870, who was a painter. They had three children Nancy 1871, Samuel 1871 (twins), and George 1874.

William died when he was thirty-one in 1874, and his son George died aged one within days of his father dying. They are both buried together in Fleetwood Cemetery (plot No D213). Once again, Lizzie was left a widow at only thirty-two. It would be interesting to know how Elizabeth felt about her life as it must have been a problematic hard life. They lived at 26 Flag Street for many years, and we know those houses were small, and with a family of seven, it must have been very cramped for them.

Lizzie did have another child in 1876 two years after William died, and at this stage, I'm not sure who the father was. Still, interestingly she called her baby Elizabeth Harrison Tilley which looks like she named the baby in memory of the two young husbands she had lost. Elizabeth married my great grandfather Thomas Rogers in 1878. Thomas was a widower, so he had also been married before. Elizabeth and Thomas were only married for eight years when Thomas had a sudden heart attack and died at age forty-eight on July 31st, 1886. Their son John Henry was only seven, and Martha was six. Lizzie never remarried after that, and she died of a cerebral haemorrhage at her home 25 Warren Street on the April 26th, 1907 age sixty-three, her daughter Ellen was with her. Ellen's married name was Greenwood, and she was living at 9 Kemp Street at the time of her mother's death. I found the story of Lizzie so sad, but I believe each of her marriages was happy, and she was loved. She lived her life, bringing up her seven children alone mainly due to the early deaths of her three husbands.

It is interesting to note on her first marriage certificate, it states her father was John Porter, a farmer, but on the next two marriage certificates, her father was named John Cowell. I can only presume she discovered who her father was as time went by. I can confirm her father was John Cowell as I have now received her birth certificate. An interesting mystery surrounding Thomas and Elizabeth's surname is that Thomas was born Thomas Rogers, and was married as Thomas Rogers. Somewhere along the way, Botham became their surname, and their surname Rogers became a middle name. The name change must have happened between their marriage in 1878 and Thomas's death in 1886 as the name on his death certificate is Thomas Rogers Botham. Up to now, I have not found any links or information as to why this happened. My Aunt Vera had the middle name of Rogers, so it appears it became a popular family name

We lived next door to Martha, who was, of course, our great Aunt Martha, and she was very stern-faced with us all, and we were a bit scared of her. Mum used to tell us off if we were too loud as Aunty Martha wouldn't like it. We never went into her house, and it seemed a bit odd to be living next door to your aunty but not having a relationship with her. At the time, of course, this fact never entered my head, but as I got older, I wondered why it appeared she didn't quite like us. I do wonder if grandad had been living things may have been different. She married William Wright and lived at number 82 Warren Street. Her daughter Margaret (Maggie) was lovely, and I have since caught up with Maggie's daughter Joan who gave me some interesting information. It appears they very much-loved Aunty

Martha, and she took on the care of some of Lizzie's grandchildren, so that was nice to know. I feel quite differently toward her now, and with knowing Lizzie's story, I am so grateful to Aunty Martha for helping where she could.

JOHN HENRY ROGERS BOTHAM
1869-1942 (my grandad) *Married Jennie Jones*

My granddad John Henry Rogers Botham, he was born at 26 Flag Street on June 9th, 1879. His father was Thomas Rogers and his mother Elizabeth Rogers late Tilley, Harrison nee Porter. His mother had been widowed twice before marrying Thomas. As I have explained at the time of his birth, his father Thomas was a boilermaker's labourer, and his surname was Rogers. After their marriage, it is interesting to note that the surname Rogers was dropped and became a middle name. Granddad went by the surname of Botham on both his marriage and death certificates also his war record even though he was a Rogers on his birth certificate. It is a bit of a mystery because I can't find out where Botham has come from, so I will have to continue my search on that one.

Granddad joined the Navy on August 25th, 1914, and was a leading seaman based in HMS Vivid Devonport down south, and that is where he married Nan. They married on March 30th, 1916, and he was ten years older than her. His dad Thomas was deceased at that time, and his profession was a fisherman. His record shows him mobilised in 1915 before having any training, sailing on the HMS Kumu He was awarded the 1914-15 Star British war medal and the Victory medal. His war/navy record showed that Granddad was only 5ft5in tall and had blue eyes with a fresh complexion. He had a tattoo on each arm, on his left was a gravestone and an anchor "In memory of my mother", and on his right arm a ship and clasped hand, across the sea. He lived with his sister Martha and her family at 82 Warren Street Fleetwood when he joined the Navy, and he demobbed in 1919.

JANE HOPE JONES (Jennie)
1892-1978 (My nan) *Married John Henry Rogers Botham*

Nan was born at Hooson's Cottage in Connah's Quay North Wales on the July 22nd, 1892. Nan's Christian name was known to us all as Jennie, but she was christened Jane Hope Jones. Aunty Myra can remember a tapestry in Aunty Edith's house in Wales that had the name Jane Hope embroidered into it, (I wonder where that is now). Her father was Richard Jones and her mother, Jane. Her paternal grandmother was named Mary Hope before she was married, so Nan bore her grandmother's surname. Nan's childhood was not perfect. Her father Richard a blacksmith, drank a lot. He threw Nan and her mother out of the home on many occasions. Because of this Nan spent a lot of her childhood in and out of the workhouse. Aunty Myra told me that nan had two sisters called Mary and Rose, and I really couldn't understand where these sisters were when Nan and her mother were in and out of the workhouse and needing help. There were lots of questions to answer and a mystery to unravel about those two sisters, and I had a feeling they were not her blood sisters, and my cousin John seemed to agree. To understand a lot of Nan's life, I will need to guide you through what I know of her sisters and maternal grandparents.

Jane's (Nans mother) father was called Henry Campbell, and he was born in Tyrone, Ireland, in about 1817, and he went to live in Manchester during the Potato Famine. He married Jane's mother in 1851, and at that time he was a widower. Her mother's name was Mary Kenny and she was also originally from Ireland. Henry was a chemical worker, and it looks like this is what took him from Manchester to Wales. In the 1871 census, Jane (Nans mum) was living with Henry and Mary in Flint. Jane had a child out of wedlock called Mary known as Campbell, when she was just sixteen. Jane married William McCluskey in 1875 and had Rose known as McCluskey, so the sisters had different fathers and were much older than Nan, which accounts for them not being around when Nan was little. William McCluskey must have died, and Jane then married Richard Jones in 1891, and they had Nan together. Her stepsister Rose was a servant age seventeen in 1891 at a hotel in Chester but went to live in Argentina as a governess. I believe she married the Ambassador to Sweden, although

I have never been able to confirm this and spent many years living in the USA during the first World War. When he died, she remarried to a man called Horace Dobson. Rose was very wealthy and had told nan she would make sure she was looked after financially when she died. Rose ended up in a nursing home in Kent and died at age ninety-two. The other sister Mary was a domestic servant for a chemical manufacturer in 1901 and then had a child out of wedlock in 1904. Mary called her Rose after her sister, but she was not kind to her, and Rose's daughter Susan told me she once told Rose that she wished she had never had her, something Rose never forgot. When I looked at the 1911 census, Mary had married William Kemp, and they had a son together, but poor Rose was in the census as a boarder, not as her daughter, something which I thought was terrible and showed the life Rose must have had. Mary died in Sheffield in 1940, age 65 years old. There is a happy ending, though, as Rose left home and went to live in London when she was only 15 and eventually met her husband, Walter Taylor, and had two daughters Rose and Susan, who now both live in America. Walter died in 1976, and Rose died in Kent in 1991. I am in touch with Susan, her daughter, and grateful to her as she helped me with Nan's story.

THE END

IT HAS BEEN A PRIVILEGE to get to know my ancestral family, and I will cherish their memory until I become one of those ancestors myself. There are not many of my generation left, and one of the sad things about getting older is seeing those we love pass away. Our family has experienced many tragedies just as those who went before us did, but we were lucky to have lived in less rigid times, and having a more accepting society. When I think of the families who have passed from generation to generation, I am amazed I didn't hear anything about them; that they had even existed. They had been forgotten to time as they were never spoke about and they had done their job of passing down genes for us to inherit. Although we do carry their genetic makeup, I believe it is the environmental influences we live alongside that shaped our lives. I do think my parents would have thought about their past families even though they never spoke about them, just as I think of my nan's and aunties. Thoughts were never enough for me, though, once I started to get those names and dates, I wanted to know more. Their lives were meaningful to me; they married, had children, experienced and faced adversary head-on just like we had done. They also had their times of sadness which is something our family never escaped from. They went to war and fought for their country with pride, and they were real people worthy of being remembered. I hope I have convinced you that there is more to writing names and dates when you are researching your family history; there are also many stories to be told.

I hope you have enjoyed some of the stories about my ancestors. There are still many more stories to discover, but I think they will have to be told by someone else. I will carry on searching for clues and adding information to my tree to help with these stories. Don't wait till you are older to become interested, even if you don't want to do your family tree, ask the questions and jot them down for anyone that might want to search in the future, now there's a challenge for you.

The following family members are the only family left from my generation level, and we still have contact and care about each other.

Janet Kemp nee Gorst
Margaret Towers nee Gorst
Harry Woods
Valerie Wilson nee Woods
Robert (Bobbie) Crowford
Joan Bond nee Crowford
Brian Crowford
John Gawne
Roger Kerr
Robert Kerr

"We're all immortal, as long as our stories are told."
Elizabeth Hunter, The Scribe

Lightning Source UK Ltd.
Milton Keynes UK
UKHW040749110722
405680UK00001B/90